MARINE INSURANCE ACT 1906 vs. INSURANCE ACT 2015

~ A Critical Comparison ~

This dissertation is submitted in partial fulfilment of the requirements for the award of the degree of Master of Laws (LL.M.), Common Professional Examination, of the University of Wolverhampton Law School in the United Kingdom.

Submitted on 28 March 2019

John L. Clark

1

DECLARATION

Whilst registered as a candidate for the foregoing degree, I was not registered for any other wholly or partially research-based award nor associated with any research institute or law society. The opinions and conclusions embodied herein are solely the author's work and have not been submitted elsewhere.

The following consists of a section-by-section critical comparison of the Marine Insurance Act 1906 and Insurance Act 2015, an analysis of the doctrine of *uberrimæ fidei* and a revision of selected cases brought before English courts both before and after the enactment of the new Act to identify a pattern of evolution towards modern adjudication of insurance matters. However, no suggestion for legislative reform is proffered herein.

ABSTRACT

The Marine Insurance Act 1906[1] contains provisions dealing specifically with maritime matters which may be directly applicable to any contract of insurance by removing or replacing certain terms. The definition of a marine insurance contract in section 1, for example, "A contract of marine insurance is a contract whereby the insurer undertakes to indemnify the assured, in manner and to the extent thereby agreed, against marine losses, that is to say, the losses incident to marine adventure," could refer to any contract simply by deleting the word "marine." The bulk of the Marine Insurance Act articulates universal concepts and principles generally applicable to the entire insurance industry, namely disclosures and representations, warranties and loss, hence its global significance in that field for over a century, and its broad implementation and transposition in the legal systems of many Commonwealth nations. But despite its meticulousness and merits, a glaring point of contention is the infamous principle of *uberrimæ fidei* (or "utmost good faith") for insurance contracts set out in section 17, "A contract of marine insurance is a contract based upon the utmost good faith, and, if the utmost good faith be not observed by either party, the contract may be avoided by the other party," which originated in 1766 based on Lord Mansfield's comments in *Carter v Boehm*:[2] "Insurance is a contract based upon speculation. The special facts, upon which the contingent chance is to be computed, lie most commonly in the knowledge of the insured only; the underwriter trusts to his representation and

---

[1] *Marine Insurance Act 1906*
[2] *Carter v Boehm 1766*

proceeds upon the confidence that he does not keep back any circumstance in his knowledge, to mislead the underwriter into a belief that the circumstance does not exist, and to induce him to estimate the risk as if it did not exist. Good faith forbids either party by concealing what he privately knows, to draw the other into a bargain from his ignorance of that fact, and his believing the contrary."

Contrastingly, in a clear effort to democratise the legal framework for insurance contracts, the Insurance Act 2015[3] enshrines the duty of fair presentation in section 3, "Before a contract of insurance is entered into, the insured must make to the insurer a fair presentation of the risk," and effectively derogated the cumbersome "utmost good faith" precept to the dustbin of history in section 14, "Any rule of law permitting a party to a contract of insurance to avoid the contract on the ground that the utmost good faith has not been observed by the other party is abolished," boldly doing away with the archaic Latin expression. The Insurance Act also concisely provides for warranties and remedies for fraud in five succinct sections and abolishes so-called "basis of the contract" clauses in section 9, "This section applies to representations made by the insured [which are] not capable of being converted into a warranty by means of any provision of the non-consumer insurance contract (or of the terms of the variation), or of any other contract (and whether by declaring the representation to form the basis of the contract or otherwise)." by prohibiting the conversion of any representation by the insured into a warranty by means of contractual

---

[3] *Insurance Act 2015*

provision, which was originally obligated in Marine Insurance Act, section 35 (2), "An express warranty must be included in, or written upon, the policy, or must be contained in some document incorporated by reference into the policy." The author will elaborate on the foregoing herein by presenting each section of the Marine Insurance Act and its relevance to corresponding sections of the Insurance Act, provide an analysis of *uberrimæ fidei* and examine cases adjudicated based on both laws before and after the 2015 modernisation.

ACKNOWLEDGEMENTS

I would like to express my sincere appreciation to the University of Wolverhampton's Head of Law School, Professor Sukhninder Panesar, for his guidance and supervision. He effectively and consistently pointed me in the right direction and provided valuable comments that positively affected my thinking process and perspective.

I am immensely grateful to Dr. Toshiaki Shimoyamada, a legend in the field of maritime law in Japan who initially sparked my interest in pursuing a legal career, as well as to Messrs. Robert Hinkel, Bert Lefever and Peter Tyksinski, Esq. for their intellectual support and encouragement, and whose ardent persuasion tactics were instrumental in my decision to take this path.

Finally, none of this would have been possible without the love and devotion of my beautiful wife, Arisa.

TABLE OF CONTENTS

BACKGROUND, OBJECTIVES AND SCOPE

My interest in maritime law was engendered some years ago whilst clerking at the chambers of Dr. Shimoyamada in Tokyo, Japan. I had the esteemed honour of assisting him in the seizure of cargo ships whose owners had committed fraud to avoid paying for bunker fuel. Awaiting ships at port and boarding them armed with court orders and accompanied by harbour police officers was quite a thrill indeed, so were the almost immediate calls from banks confirming the remittance of the funds in arrears. During our time together, he graciously included me in fascinating meetings with the representatives of global shipping companies, ship registrars, insurance brokers and more. I will never forget his generosity, broad insight and expertise, and his peculiar maritime-themed cufflinks featuring anchors, tillers, tall ships, etc.

Due to the importance for any lawyer of a strong comprehension of insurance law, the landmark cases that cite the Marine Insurance Act, and the modern and progressive legal concepts articulated in the Insurance Act, the scope of this dissertation was narrowed to an academic exercise constituting a critical comparison thereof with a focus on maritime affairs, specifically from the perspective of the relevance of the former in the modern era of insurance as embodied by the latter, a conjecture as to how verdicts evolved post-modernisation, meaning after the passage of the Insurance Act, and an analysis of the principle of *uberrimæ fidei*.

IMPORTANCE AND CONTRIBUTION

The importance and contribution of this study lay in potentially providing an approach to litigators involved in claims based on retroactive insurance contracts that cover losses after their occurrence, such as the so-called *incurred but not reported* (IBNR) claims by enterprises that were self-insured prior to 2016 or other general backdated liability claims, or loss mitigation underwriting designed to cover a loss event that occurred prior to 2016 when the Marine Insurance Act was still in force but whose magnitude had yet to be determined after the Insurance Act was promulgated. This may open the door to retroaction that could potentially lead to reparations or compensation benefiting either counterparty or a third party.

Moreover, whilst a clear overestimation of this study's importance to posterity, perhaps a group of tech-savvy youngsters will one day find inspiration from these pages and develop some sort of legal artificial intelligence capable of applying new legislation to old cases in hopes of righting historical wrongs or resolving outstanding issues spanning decades.

RELEVANCE OF MARINE INSURANCE ACT SECTIONS 1 TO 16

The Marine Insurance Act starts off with a benign definition of marine insurance contract in section 1, "A contract of marine insurance is a contract whereby the insurer undertakes to indemnify the assured, in manner and to the extent thereby agreed, against marine losses, that is to say, the losses incident to marine adventure," which was replaced in the Insurance Act with five basic definitions for consumer and non-consumer insurance contracts, the insured (doing away with the term "assured") and the insurer, and, straight away, the duty of fair presentation, for which the next seven sections are devoted. Indeed, 21st century legislators wasted no time to steer us away from the infamous *uberrimæ fidei*. Interestingly, although the bulk of Marine Insurance Act provisions are generally applicable to any insurance contract either as specific maritime provisions whose references to seagoing vessels, cargoes, equipment, masters and crew, harbours and voyages are deleted or replaced with neutral terms, or as clearly articulated universal principles, section 2 (2), "Where a ship in course of building, or the launch of a ship, or any adventure analogous to a marine adventure, is covered by a policy in the form of a marine policy, the provisions of this Act, in so far as applicable, shall apply thereto; but, except as by this section provided, nothing in this Act shall alter or affect any rule of law applicable to any contract of insurance other than a contract of marine insurance as by this Act defined," draws a stark distinction between "any insurance contract" and "a contract of marine insurance" declaring them mutually exclusive in terms of the Marine Insurance Act's applicability.

The definitions of insurable property and maritime adventure in Marine Insurance Act, section 3, "(a) Any ship goods or other movables are exposed to maritime perils. Such property is in this Act referred to as 'insurable property'; (b) The earning or acquisition of any freight, passage money, commission, profit, or other pecuniary benefit, or the security for any advances, loan, or disbursements, is endangered by the exposure of insurable property to maritime perils; (c) Any liability to a third party may be incurred by the owner of, or other person interested in or responsible for, insurable property, by reason of maritime perils. 'Maritime perils' means the perils consequent on, or incidental to, the navigation of the sea, that is to say, perils of the seas, fire, war perils, pirates, rovers, thieves, captures, seizures, restraints, and detainments of princes and peoples, jettisons, barratry, and any other perils, either of the like kind or which may be designated by the policy," were stricken in the Insurance Act, whilst the elaboration of "maritime perils" therein to include pirates, rovers, detainments of princes and barratry is laughable in a 21st century context, unless the reader happens to be Somalian, as are wagering or gaming insurance contracts in section 4, "Every contract of marine insurance by way of gaming or wagering is void," therein defined as "where the assured has not an insurable interest [and] the contract is entered into with no expectation of acquiring such an interest," further explained as "without the benefit of salvage."

The Insurance Act does not refer to "perils" but rather "risks" specifically in terms of how they are presented to the insurer based on the knowledge thereof possessed by the insured. This is the essence of the duty of fair representation articulated in the Insurance Act, section

3 as: "Before a contract of insurance is entered into, the insured must make to the insurer a fair presentation of the risk [which] makes that disclosure in a manner which would be reasonably clear and accessible to a prudent insurer, and in which every material representation as to a matter of fact is substantially correct, and every material representation as to a matter of expectation or belief is made in good faith [whereby the] disclosure of every material circumstance which the insured knows, is presumed to know or ought to know, or, failing that, disclosure which gives the insurer sufficient information to put a prudent insurer on notice that it needs to make further enquiries for the purpose of revealing those material circumstances."

Whilst "insurable interest" is concisely defined in Marine Insurance Act, section 5, "(1) Subject to the provisions of this Act, every person has an insurable interest who is interested in a marine adventure; (2) In particular a person is interested in a marine adventure where he stands in any legal or equitable relation to the adventure or to any insurable property at risk therein, in consequence of which he may benefit by the safety or due arrival of insurable property, or may be prejudiced by its loss, or by damage thereto, or by the detention thereof, or may incur liability in respect thereof," the following three sections are unnecessary attempts to elaborate on when, in terms of the specific time of the loss event, an assured party must be interested in the subject-matter insured as an insurable interest in order to recover, and on what type of interest, whether defeasible, contingent or partial, is insurable (the example provided in Marine Insurance Act, section 7 (2), "In particular, where the buyer of goods has insured them, he has an insurable interest, notwithstanding that he might, at his election, have rejected the goods, or have treated them as at the seller's risk, by reason of the latter's delay in making delivery or otherwise," on the treatment of goods is absolutely moot). The Insurance Act eradicates these provisions altogether. The provisions on reinsurance in Marine Insurance Act, section 9, "(1) The insurer under a contract of marine insurance has an insurable interest in his risk, and may re-insure in respect of it; (2) Unless the policy otherwise provides, the original assured has no right or interest in respect of such re-insurance," are transposed in the form of a minute mention in Insurance Act, section 4 (5) (b), "if the contract re-insures risks covered by another contract, the persons who are (by virtue of this subsection) connected with that other contract," which simply defines the persons connected with a contract of reinsurance. The Marine Insurance Act, section 10 on "bottomry" and "respondentia" bonds, "The lender of money on bottomry or respondentia has an insurable interest in respect of the loan," both archaic forms of liens on ships or cargoes, as insurable interest should have been included in some modern form in the Insurance Act before being stricken as useless vestiges of a bygone era. Ditto for master and seamen wages, "The master or any member of the crew of a ship has an insurable interest in respect of his wages," advance freight, "In the case of advance freight, the person advancing the freight has an insurable interest, in so far as such freight is not repayable in case of loss," and the next three Marine Insurance Act sections on charges, "The assured has an insurable interest in the charges of any insurance which he may effect," equitable interest in mortgages and indemnity, "(1) Where the subject-matter insured is mortgaged, the mortgagor has an insurable interest in the full value thereof, and the mortgagee has an insurable interest in respect of any sum due or to become due under the mortgage," and assignment of interest, "Where the assured assigns or otherwise parts with his interest in the subject-matter insured, he does not thereby transfer to the assignee his rights under the contract of insurance, unless there be an express or implied agreement with the assignee to that effect. But the provisions of this section do not affect a transmission of interest by operation of law." The determination of insurable value in Marine Insurance Act, section 16, "(1) In insurance on ship, the insurable value is the value, at the commencement of the risk, of the ship, including her outfit, provisions and stores for the officers and crew, money advanced for seamen's wages, and other disbursements (if any) incurred to make the ship fit for the voyage or adventure contemplated by the policy, plus the charges of insurance upon the whole: The insurable value, in the case of a steamship, includes also the machinery, boilers, and coals and engine stores if owned by the assured, and, in the case of a ship engaged in a special trade, the ordinary fittings requisite for that trade: (2) In insurance on freight, whether paid in advance or otherwise, the insurable value is the gross amount of the freight at the risk of the assured, plus the charges of insurance: (3) In insurance on goods or merchandise, the insurable value is the prime cost of the property insured, plus the expenses of and incidental to shipping and the charges of insurance upon the whole: (4) In insurance on any other subject-matter, the insurable value is the amount at the risk of the assured when the policy attaches, plus the charges of insurance," was stricken as it deals specifically with ships and freight, etc.

The notion of insuring subject-matter based on its value at the commencement of the risk ("In insurance on ship, the insurable value is the value, at the commencement of the risk, of the ship, including her outfit, provisions and stores for the officers and crew, money advanced for seamen's wages, and other disbursements (if any) incurred to make the ship fit for the voyage or adventure contemplated by the policy, plus the charges of insurance upon the whole.") was abolished in Insurance Act, section 11, which outlaws any insurance contract term not "defining the risk as a whole [such as] a loss of a particular kind [or] at a particular location [or] time."

Quite contrastingly, the next five sections on disclosure and representations, most of which were carried into the Insurance Act except *uberrimæ fidei*, are universal in terms of applicability to modern insurance contracts.

UBERRIMÆ FIDEI VS. DUTY OF FAIR PRESENTATION

Marine Insurance Act, section 17, "A contract of marine insurance is a contract upon the utmost good faith, and if the utmost good faith be not observed by either party, the contract may be avoided by the other party," bluntly equates insurance with *uberrimæ fidei* ("utmost good faith") as mutually exclusive, effectively arming insurers with the power to nullify any contract should a representation by an insured party be proven false regarding the subject-matter insured or claim regardless of intent or prior knowledge. This was the law of the land for 106 years until the Consumer Insurance (Disclosure and Representations) Act (2012),[4] section 2 (2) replaced it with "the duty to take reasonable care not to make a misrepresentation to the insurer," which was subsequently expanded in 2015 with the elaborate "duty of fair presentation" enshrined in Insurance Act, sections 3 to 8, summarised above. Most compelling is the wording of Marine Insurance Act, section 18. Legislators in 1906 deemed it appropriate to require the insured to "disclose every material circumstance" known thereto, as he is by law "deemed to know every circumstance" of his affairs or face potential nullification (i.e. the prerogative of the insurer to "avoid the contract"). A "circumstance," which according to section 18 (5) includes any communication or information made or proffered to or from the insured, is material if the insurer is influenced thereby in the course of deciding whether to assume the risk or of pricing the insurance contract. This notion is extended to insurance agents acting on behalf of the

---

[4] *Consumer Insurance (Disclosure and Representations) Act (2012)*

insured in section 19, "Subject to the provisions of the preceding section as to circumstances which need not be disclosed, where an insurance is effected for the assured by an agent, the agent must disclose to the insurer: (a) Every material circumstance which is known to himself, and an agent to insure is deemed to know every circumstance which in the ordinary course of business ought to be known by, or to have been communicated to, him; and (b) Every material circumstance which the assured is bound to disclose, unless it come to his knowledge too late to communicate it to the agent."

Interestingly, Marine Insurance Act, section 20 (4), "A representation as to a matter of fact is true, if it be substantially correct, that is to say, if the difference between what is represented and what is actually correct would not be considered material by a prudent insurer," articulates the peculiar "principle of substantial correctness," a term coined by the author, with respect to representations as to fact on the part of the insured, declaring that such a representation is true if it be "substantially correct," i.e. free of any material discrepancy between that which is represented by the insured and what is actually correct all, of course, from the lofty perspective of the "prudent insurer." The next subsection, section 20 (5), comically declares – in true *Trumpian* fashion – that, as an alternative to fact, a representation of "expectation or belief" is true when made in good faith, "A representation as to a matter of expectation or belief is true if it be made in good faith." This not only conflicts with *uberrimæ fidei* enshrined just a few sections above but also propounds a new genre of deceit, albeit unintended, specific to insurance contracts that, whilst not tortious per common law, results from a mistake in the comprehension of a certain circumstance, expectation or belief as it is represented or communicated to the insurer prior to contracting and on which a claim is subsequently relied upon, whose sanction ultimately is contract avoidance.

Insurance Act, section 3 casts away the rigidity and unforgiveness of the past and instead requires merely a "fair presentation" of the risk by the insured through disclosure of material circumstances that are "reasonably clear and accessible" to the insurer providing him with sufficient knowledge that triggers "further enquiries for the purpose of revealing" such circumstances. The onus, therefore, is now on both parties to uncover all the aspects of the subject-matter insured. Interestingly, legislators transposed into Insurance Act, section 3 (3) (c), "A fair presentation of the risk is one in which every material representation as to a matter of fact is substantially correct, and every material representation as to a matter of expectation or belief is made in good faith," the peculiar obligation of substantial correctness of material representation as to fact, whose definition is stealthily provided down below in section 7 (5), "A material representation is substantially correct if a prudent insurer would not consider the difference between what is represented and what is actually correct to be material," and identical to Marine Insurance Act, section 20 (4), but shrewdly rewrote Marine Insurance Act, section 20 (5), which declared that any expectation or belief is "true" if made in good faith, as mentioned above, establishing instead that any such representation "would be considered a fair presentation of a risk" if made in good faith.

Insurance Act, section 4 deals specifically with the knowledge of the insured party, i.e. what he knows or ought to know or what is known by him or anyone responsible for his insurance, who is defined as any individual involved in the procurement of insurance on behalf of the insured, any employee of such agent, or senior management personnel of the insured. Section 5 outlines what constitutes the knowledge of the insurer, which is simply what is known to him or those making the decision to assume the risk on behalf of the insurer, and describes what he "ought to know" as what information should have reasonably been passed on thereto, and what he is "presumed to know" as common knowledge and information he is reasonably expected to know in the ordinary course of business. These two sections are transpositions of Marine Insurance Act, sections 18 and 19, respectively, dealing with disclosure. The next section, Insurance Act, section 6, "For the purposes of sections 3 to 5, references to an individual's knowledge include not only actual knowledge, but also matters which the individual suspected, and of which the individual would have had knowledge but for deliberately refraining from confirming them or enquiring about them," invents a new type of knowledge defined as what is suspected and what would have been known but for "deliberately refraining from confirming or enquiring," presumably due to the exercise of faith to some degree by one party taking the other at his word.

The remedies for breach of fair representation in Insurance Act, section 8 have no precedent in the Marine Insurance Act. In case of a misrepresentation in an insurance contract, the insurer must demonstrate that the contract would never have been entered into or would have been forged under different terms *sine qua non* (but for) the misrep, which must be a so-called "qualifying breach," which must be proven by the insurer as deliberate or reckless on the part of the insured. Subsection 6 places the burden of proof squarely on the shoulders of the insurer, "It is for the insurer to show that a qualifying breach was deliberate or reckless," requiring him to demonstrate that the insured either "knew that it was in breach of the duty of fair presentation" or "did not care whether or not it was in breach of that duty" in order to justify the nullification of a claim. The Insurance Act, Schedule 1 is a laundry list of insurer remedies for qualifying breaches, which include avoidance of the contract, refusal of claim, refusal to return premiums paid, proportionate reduction of amount payable on a claim, among others specifically conceived to protect the insured from arbitrary denial of claims as well as the insurer from deliberate or reckless breaches. Protections afforded to both counterparties to insurance contracts are a stark departure from the spartan and unforgiving Marine Insurance Act exclusions and limitations of insurer liability at the expense of the insured.

WARRANTIES

In comparison with the meagre section 9 in the Insurance Act on warranties and representations consisting only of a clause forbidding the conversion of a representation into a warranty by provision of any contract, insurance or otherwise, the topic is covered at length in Marine Insurance Act, sections 33 to 35. Not only is there an elaborate definition of a promissory warranty, "(1) A warranty, in the following sections relating to warranties, means a promissory warranty, that is to say, a warranty by which the assured undertakes that some particular thing shall or shall not be done, or that some condition shall be fulfilled, or whereby he affirms or negatives the existence of a particular state of facts," as an expressed or implied affirmation or negation of some action, condition or state of facts to be "exactly complied with" regardless of whether material or immaterial to the risk or else the insurer is "discharged from liability" and the insured is not allowed to provide evidence of remedy and compliance in his defence against the insurer's claim of breach of warranty (section 34-2), "Where a warranty is broken, the assured cannot avail himself of the defence that the breach has been remedied, and the warranty complied with, before loss." As previously indicated herein, section 35 obliges insurers to include express warranties in the insurance policy or appendix thereto. This was abolished in the Insurance Act, as per the foregoing section 9. The remaining six sections on warranties in the Marine Insurance Act specifically deal with war, ships, cargoes and voyages, provisions that were obliterated in 2015.

Regarding breach of warranty, the aforementioned Marine Insurance Act, section 34-2 is effectively rewritten in Insurance Act, section 10-2, "An insurer has no liability under a contract of insurance in respect of any loss occurring, or attributable to something happening, after a warranty (express or implied) in the contract has been breached but before the breach has been remedied," to allow a breach to be remedied but removes insurer liability over the period between the breach and the remedy. This democratisation is clarified in Insurance Act, section 4, "Subsection (2) does not affect the liability of the insurer in respect of losses occurring, or attributable to something happening (a) before the breach of warranty, or (b) if the breach can be remedied, after it has been remedied," effectively articulating the period of lawful coverage (i.e. insurer liability) as before the breach and after the remedy. Where the Marine Insurance Act permitted an insurer to cancel a policy in the event of any breach as a violation of *uberrimæ fidei*, notwithstanding losses prior to the discovery thereof (section 33-3), "(3) A warranty, as above defined, is a condition which must be exactly complied with, whether it be material to the risk or not. If it be not so complied with, then, subject to any express provision in the policy, the insurer is discharged from liability as from the date of the breach of warranty, but without prejudice to any liability incurred by him before that date," the Insurance Act abolishes this clause in section 10-7, "In the Marine Insurance Act 1906, (a) in section 33 (nature of warranty), in subsection (3), the second sentence is omitted, (b) section 34 (when breach of warranty excused) is omitted."

Lastly, the eleven Marine Insurance Act sections in the chapters entitled "Warranties, etc." and "The Voyage" (sections 39 to 49) regarding particular objects such as ships, equipment, goods and movables, particular locations such as harbours, ports or the open sea, and specific times such as commencement of the risk or voyage (romantically described as the "adventure") at the departure point, the different stages of the same including ports of discharge, and the destination, are abolished in Insurance Act, section 11-1, "This section applies to a term (express or implied) of a contract of insurance, other than a term defining the risk as a whole, if compliance with it would tend to reduce the risk of one or more of the following (a) loss of a particular kind, (b) loss at a particular location, (c) loss at a particular time." That section's other three subsections effectively reinforce section 10, as described above, assuring coverage to the insured even in case of breach of warranty if he satisfies that the same could not have increased the risk of the loss, and forbidding the insurer to rely thereon to "exclude, limit or discharge its liability under the contract" for that loss. This is arguably the final nail in the coffin of *uberrimæ fidei*.

LOSS, ABANDONMENT & ABROGATION

The Marine Insurance Act contains some two dozen sections on loss that were stricken in the new law. Early 20th century legislators deemed it necessary to define loss and provide specific, albeit simplistic and obvious, guidelines regarding attribution and liability that 21st century framers completely ignored. The first Marine Insurance Act section on loss, section 55, makes the insurer liable for "any loss proximately caused by a peril insured against," which is reasonable. Although there is no liability for losses incurred as a result of the wilful misconduct of the insured, the insurer is nonetheless liable for a loss insured against that "would not have happened but for [such] misconduct or negligence" (55-2 (a)). The next two subsections of 55 deal specifically with ships. 55-2 (b) protects insurers against losses caused by shipment delays, even those resulting from a risk covered in the policy, and (c) indemnifies against ordinary wear and tear, leakage, breakage, rats or vermin, and, quite interestingly, any inherent vice or nature of the subject-matter insured, "Unless the policy otherwise provides, the insurer on ship or goods is not liable for any loss proximately caused by delay, although the delay be caused by a peril insured against." This last clause means that a party would enter into an insurance contract to insure a specific subject-matter whose inherent vice or nature would, if resulting in loss, exempt the insurer, "Unless the policy otherwise provides, the insurer is not liable for ordinary wear and tear, ordinary leakage and breakage, inherent vice or nature of the subject-matter insured, or for any loss proximately caused by rats or vermin, or for any injury to machinery not proximately caused by maritime perils."

The next several sections clearly define partial loss, actual total loss and constructive total loss, and the effects thereof on the outcome of a claim. What is confusing, however, is the relationship between actual total loss and abandonment as outlined in the following sections, and the resulting arbitrary entitlement afforded to the insurer in the old law. Whilst actual total loss is clearly defined in Marine Insurance Act, section 57 as destruction or damage of the subject-matter insured to the extent where it "ceases to be a thing of the kind insured, or where the assured is irretrievably deprived thereof," assumingly as a result of piracy on the high seas or seizure by some irate potentate, there is no mention of abandonment, except to say that notice thereof is unnecessary in case of actual total loss. It is not until the definition of constructive actual loss in section 60 does the correlation with abandonment appear in the clause "reasonably abandoned on account of its actual total loss [whereby] it could not be preserved [therefrom] without an expenditure which would exceed its value." And again, in section 61: "Where there is a constructive total loss the assured may either treat the loss as a partial loss, or abandon the subject-matter insured to the insurer and treat the loss as if it were an actual total loss." This is important to note because of the so-called "effect of abandonment" stipulated in section 63 where, in the event of abandonment by the insured subsequent to a claim of actual total loss, "the insurer is entitled to take over the interest of the assured in whatever may remain of the subject-matter insured, and all proprietary rights incidental thereto."

Therefore, actual total loss is clear and evident loss, whilst a constructive total loss can be treated by the insured as a partial loss or an actual total loss whereby the object insured is abandoned and ownership therein is vested in the insurer, with consideration therefor presumably constituted as the insurance benefits payable on the claim. Section 62 does nevertheless stipulate that abandonment and the resulting vestment occurs in the event "the assured elects to abandon the subject-matter insured," thus affording some protection to the policyholder, however, section 79-1 effectively upends this right as it provides the insurer with the right of subrogation where. if he "pays for a total loss…he thereupon becomes entitled to take over the interest of the assured in whatever may remain of the subject-matter so paid for, and he is thereby subrogated to all the rights and remedies of the assured in and in respect of that subject-matter as from the time of the casualty causing the loss." As if that weren't bad enough, the Marine Insurance Act legislators felt obliged to add insult to injury in subsection 2 which deals with subrogation in the event of a partial loss where, if "the insurer pays for a partial loss, he acquires no title to the subject-matter insured, or such part of it as may remain, but he is thereupon subrogated to all rights and remedies of the assured in and in respect of the subject-matter insured as from the time of the casualty causing the loss, in so far as the assured has been indemnified, according to this Act, by such payment for the loss." Therefore, ownership in the subject-matter insured is vested to the insurer in addition to all the rights and remedies of the insured in case of an actual total loss, but not a partial loss whereupon the insurer merely acquires all rights and remedies. This is an arbitrary entitlement to property arising simply by accepting a claim and covering the loss through payment of insurance benefits per the contract whereafter the subject-matter insured becomes the asset of the insurance company. It is no wonder that 21st century legislators chose to abolish these clauses as they clearly place the insured at a disadvantage and promote the enrichment of insurance companies at the expense thereof not only through the payment of premiums but also the takeover of assets in case of abandonment.

Lastly, the provisions on particular and general average loss and their incidentals, namely Marine Insurance Act, sections 64, 66 and 76, are dumbfounding as a semantic exercise in minutiæ articulation by seemingly astute legislators, which were rightfully stricken in 2015. Section 64 starts the reader off benignly with a simple definition of particular average loss as a partial loss specifically "of the subject-matter insured, caused by a peril insured against." Subsection 2 thereof provides for expenses incurred to secure and preserve the subject-matter insured as "particular charges" which are not included in the particular average. Quite straightforward. However, section 66, while entitled "General average loss," drifts into the surreal veering away from the foregoing comprehensible "Particular average loss = Partial loss" equation. Therein, general average loss is defined not as a "general loss" akin to actual total loss but rather as "a general average act" that includes a "general average expenditure as well as a general average sacrifice." Subsection 2 defines "general average act" as "any extraordinary sacrifice or expenditure voluntarily and reasonably made or incurred in time of peril for the purpose of preserving the property imperilled in the common adventure" whereby, per subsection 3, the victim is "entitled [to] a rateable contribution from the other parties interested [called] a general average contribution" and, per subsection 4, "he may recover from the insurer in respect of the proportion of the loss which falls upon him." There's a lot to digest here, but rather than providing safeguards for voluntary and reasonable sacrifices by interested parties in common adventures, wouldn't it have been simpler merely to invoke the principles of fairness, morality and equity in multi-party contracting? Whilst this "right of contribution" bestowed onto the insured in the latter subsection was duly abolished in 2015, the notion of insurer liability for the proportion of a loss incurred by the insured relative to that of other interested parties is comparable to Insurance Act, section 13-1 (b) on remedies for fraudulent claims in group insurance where "the contract provides cover for one or more other persons who are not parties to the contract, whether or not it also provides cover of any kind for [the policyholder] or another insured party."

ORIGIN OF UBERRIMÆ FIDEI

In *Manifest Shipping Company Limited v. Uni-Polaris Shipping Company Limited and Others (2001),*[5] Lord Hobhouse sheds light upon the true origin of the concept of good faith in relation to the law of insurance that stretches beyond the phrase in the judgement passed down by Lord Mansfield in *Carter v Boehm (1766)*, as provided above herein. That articulation was introduced into commercial law a general principle of good faith but unfortunately it only survived to this day in partnership and insurance contracts. With regard to the latter, Lod Mansfield considered insurance contracts as based on "speculation" due to "the inequality of information as between the proposer and the underwriter and [he] equated non-disclosure to fraud." However, whilst he did not go so far as equate non-disclosure in insurance matters to "fraudulent intention" in common law, and recognised that "keeping back" information even by mistake still takes advantage of the insurer who is nonetheless deceived and therefore entitled to avoid the contract. In *Pawson v Watson (1778),*[6] Lord Mansfield emphasised that "all dealings must be fair and honest, fraud infects and vitiates every mercantile contract. Therefore, if there is fraud in a representation, it will avoid the policy."

Almost a century later in *Bates v Hewitt (1867),*[7] Lord Cockburn reinforced Lord Mansfield's approach stating quite patriotically: "If we were to sanction such non-disclosure, especially in these days, when parties frequently forget the old rules of mercantile faith and honour

---

[5] *Manifest Shipping Company Limited v. Uni-Polaris Shipping Company Limited and Others (2001)*
[6] *Pawson v Watson (1778)*
[7] *Bates v Hewitt (1867)*

which used to distinguish this country from any other, we should be lending ourselves to innovations of a dangerous and monstrous character, which I think we ought not to do." In the opinion of the author, it is likely this pride for the accomplishments of Great Britain and the distinctive character of the British people as honest brokers with a penchant for good faith in all dealings that led 19th century legislators to go a step beyond Lord Mansfield's intention and add "utmost" to "good faith" and thus the principle of *uberrimæ fidei* was born. The latter Latin phrase may, as Lord Hobhouse points out, Title 37, Book IV of the Codex of Justinian in relation to the contract of partnership."[8]

Even more weight was added to Lord Mansfield's principle by Lord Atkin in *Bell v Lever Bros. (1932)*[9] who stated that "ordinarily the failure to disclose a material fact which might influence the mind of a prudent contractor does not give the right to avoid the contract. The principle of caveat emptor applies outside contracts of sale. There are certain contracts expressed by the law to be contracts of the utmost good faith, where material facts must be disclosed; if not, the contract is voidable. Apart from special fiduciary relationships, contracts for partnership and contracts of insurance are the leading instances. In such cases the duty does not arise out of contract; the duty of a person proposing an insurance arises before a contract is made, so of an intending partner."

The conceptual basis of utmost good faith, therefore, is absolute honesty prior to the consummation of a commercial relationship stemming from the notion that a contract

---

[8] *Bell v Lever Bros. (1932)*
[9] *Versloot Dredging BV & Anor v HDI Gerling Industrie Versicherung AG & Ors (2016)*

would take a different form, constitute different terms and conditions or would not have been executed at all in the first place had certain circumstances been revealed at the onset. Being privy to hidden defects or conditions deliberately obfuscated from a counterparty carries the penalty of contact avoidance ab initio as a deterrent for others venturing into business relations.

The proceeding paragraphs will explore how certain claims brought before English courts were adjudicated based on the judicial exercise of ascertaining the degree of knowledge of the claimant in insurance related litigation reminiscent of the popular phrase coined during the Nixon Administration's Watergate scandal by Senator Howard Baker: "What did the president know, and when did he know it."

PRIVITY VS. BLIND-EYE KNOWLEDGE

In the House of Lords case *Manifest Shipping Company Limited v Uni-Polaris Shipping Company Limited and Others (2001)*, cited above, the shipowner took out a time policy of insurance on his ship, the "Star Sea," which had been laid up in its off season. Whilst its safety certificates had been renewed before it set out to sea, it was severely damaged by fire and the shipowner filed a notice of abandonment with the underwriters claiming a constructive total loss. In their defence of their decision to dishonour the notice, the latter asserted that the ship was unseaworthy, that that state had been known to the shipowner, that the master and crew onboard had had "blind-eye knowledge" of the factors that rendered the ship unseaworthy, and that that had been causative of the fire. In his rebuke of the underwriters' claims, Lord Clyde stated that, according to Marine Insurance Act, section 39 (5), the insured would have had to prove the "privity of the assured" in sending the ship to sea "in an unseaworthy state," and that blind-eye knowledge requires a conscious reason for blinding the eye and "at least a suspicion of a truth about which you do not want to know and which you refuse to investigate, [hence] a positive decision not to look." Failing to establish such a state of mind on the part of the shipowner, their claim was thus rejected. Privity is positive knowledge aforethought and, per Marine Insurance Act, section 18, the insured had the obligation under uberrimæ fidei to disclose any and all material circumstances that he knew, was deemed to have known, and ought to have known with regard to the subject-matter insured in the course of negotiations prior to signing and sealing the insurance contract. Based on the evidence, the shipowner demonstrably lacked the "dishonest state of mind" required for liability and the underwriters, failing to prove otherwise, appealed to a higher court with a new defence claiming that, after litigation had commenced, the insured had failed to make proper disclosure of the state of the ship and true circumstances leading to the fire outbreak thus vitiating the entire contract per Marine Insurance Act, section 17. Since uberrimæ fidei is limited to pre-contractual disclosures, the law seems to allow some leeway at the latter claim filing and dispute resolution stages of the contractual relationship of the counterparties well after a peril insured against had been actualised resulting in loss, whether it be partial or total. But this cannot be the case. In stating categorically that insurance is uberrimæ fidei, section 17 requires that an element of good faith be observed throughout the period of the contractual relationship imposing duties of disclosure at all stages, not merely prior to execution, but section 18 expressly implies an extremely high degree of openness at the contract formation stage.

As a compliment to the foregoing argument by Lord Clyde, Lord Woodborough pointed out the fact that, since the insurance contract in question was a time policy, and not a voyage policy, Marine Insurance Act, section 39 (5) provides that "in a time policy there is no implied warranty that the ship shall be seaworthy at any stage of the adventure" and the insured would only be "liable for any loss attributable to unseaworthiness" if the same had been privy to such state when casting her out to sea. For the underwriters to win their case and be entitled to contract avoidance ab initio, therefore, there must have been a state of unseaworthiness at the time the vessel set sail, which must have been causative of the relevant loss, and the assured must have been privy to sending the ship to sea in that condition. Also, establishing a defence under section 17 would require proving that fraud had been perpetrated by the shipowner. But since he had acted with an honest belief that it was a claim that he was entitled to make, and since fraud is the only cause that would trigger the remedy afforded under that section, i.e. complete vitiation ab initio, the underwriters' case fell apart.

Thus, in *Uni-Polaris*, Lords Clyde and Woodborough shot gaping holes in the legal concepts buttressing the Marine Insurance Act and shone a spotlight on three key sections to undermine the arguments brandished by a group of underwriters looking to deny a shipowner's claim and avoid liability. The principle of uberrimæ fidei enshrined in section 17 and the required timeframe set forth in section 18 for disclosing the material circumstances of the subject-matter insured, which consists specifically of what the insured knew, what he was deemed to know in the course of his business, and what had ought to know, in compliance with 17 as during the pre-contractual negotiations up to the conclusion of the contract encapsulates the insured's obligation for openness, fair dealing and utmost good faith before the risk insured for is even undertaken and shields him from any accusation of fraud or obfuscation vis-à-vis an insurer or even of "turning a blind eye" to any factor that would lead to damage resulting in a partial or total loss covered by the policy, as was the case in *Uni-Polaris*, at the stage later on in the contractual relationship such as when a claim is filed for compensation or during litigation proceedings.

Section 39-5, therefore, with its precondition of "privity" on the part of the insured of a certain state or condition of the subject-matter insured, i.e. "unseaworthiness," nullifies itself if the defendant in a suit should recognise the observance of utmost good faith on the part the claimant at the time when the contract was formed.

Since 21st century legislators did away with adventures and ships and implied warranties at different stages of a risk covered by an insurance policy, the Insurance Act only focuses on knowledge and the fair representation thereof.

ESSENCE OF FRAUD

In the Supreme Court case of *Versloot Dredging BV & Anor v HDI Gerling Industrie Versicherung AG & Ors (2016)*,[10] Lord Sumption stated in his judgement that "at common law, if an insured makes a fraudulent claim on his insurer, the latter is not liable to pay the claim. The question at issue on this appeal is what constitutes a fraudulent claim. This is a controversial question at common law, which the Act of 2015 does not resolve." The matter before the court in this case involved a claim made to an insurer that was entirely justified, but the evidentiary information provided by the insured was "dishonestly embellished, either because the insured was unaware of the strength of his case or else with a view to obtaining payment faster and with less hassle." Lord Sumption did not wish to call such embellishments "fraudulent devices," as the insured did not commit fraud in presenting his claim and therefore did not conjure any devices to support it, but rather "collateral lies" which he defined as "lies which turn out when the facts are found to have no relevance to the insured's right to recover." The judgement sought in this case was to determine whether the insurer is entitled to avoid a claim supported by collateral lies if found to be irrelevant and ineffectual to the recoverability of the claim.

The claim in question involved the incapacitation of the cargo ship DC Merwestone off the coast of Lithuania due to an ingress of water that flooded the engine due partially to crew and contractor negligence, damage to certain equipment due to freezing and pumping

---

[10] *Britton v Royal Insurance Co (1866)*

system defects which rendered the main engine a constructive total loss as it was left damaged beyond repair by this event. An investigation by the solicitors for the insurer revealed that one of the ship's managers had lied as to the cause of the flooding and events immediately following its discovery on the ship because "he believed that it would fortify the claim and accelerate payment if the casualty could be blamed on the crew's failure to respond to the activation of the bilge alarm [otherwise] attention would be concentrated on the defective condition of the ship and on the possible responsibility of the owners for that state of affairs."

Whilst the appeal to the Supreme Court occurred after 2015, the event at sea occurred in 2010 and therefore Popplewell J, presiding over the court of first instance, held that, per the Marine Insurance Act, while the loss was "proximately caused by a peril of the seas, namely the fortuitous entry of seawater through the sea inlet valve during the voyage [thus negating] the contention that the owners had sent the vessel to sea with defective engine room pumps in breach of the warranty implied by section 39 (5) of the Marine Insurance Act 1906, because the managers had not known of the problem at the relevant time," the collateral lie by the manager proffered in the claim purporting to a failure to act by the crew upon bilge alarm activation, which never happened, while irrelevant to the validity of the claim and not consisting of tortious intentional fraud of any kind, was nonetheless a clear breach of *uberrimæ fidei* as established in Marine Insurance Act, section 17, therefore sinking the shipowner's valid claim of some €3.2 million. The case law is unfortunately and regrettably clear on this point. In *Britton v Royal Insurance Co (1866)*[11] Judge Willes stated that "if the claim is fraudulent, it is defeated altogether" but if the claim is valid but exaggerated or embellished seeking "to recover more than he is entitled to, that would be a wilful fraud, and the consequence is that he could not recover anything. This is a defence quite different from that of wilful arson. The law is, that a person who has made such a fraudulent claim could not be permitted to recover at all. The contract of insurance is one of perfect good faith on both sides, and it is most important that such good faith should be maintained." English courts persistently applied *Britton* throughout the 20th century and reaffirmed it in *Uni-Polaris*, but Scotland's courts followed the fairer path chartered by the learned judges of the Court of Session in *Reid & Co Ltd v Employer's Accident & Livestock Insurance Co Ltd (1899)*[12] wherein it was held that "the genuine part of a fraudulently inflated claim was recoverable." In *Uni-Polaris*, Lord Hobhouse stated that "if it is a manifestation of the duty of utmost good faith, then the effect of section 17 of the Marine Insurance Act 1906 is that the whole contract is voidable ab initio upon a breach, and not just the fraudulent claim." The enshrinement of that duty in section 17, therefore, was an attempt to deter fraud, "the logic is simple, the fraudulent insured must not be allowed to think: if the fraud is successful, then I will gain; if it is unsuccessful, I will lose nothing" (Lord Hobhouse).

---

[11] *Reid & Co Ltd v Employer's Accident & Livestock Insurance Co Ltd (1899)*
[12] *Mutual Energy Ltd v Starr Underwriting Agents Ltd & Anor (2016)*

Lord Hughes added to Lord Sumption's statement in *Versloot Dredging* stating that Insurance Act, section 12, "Remedies for fraudulent claims; (1) If the insured makes a fraudulent claim under a contract of insurance: (a) the insurer is not liable to pay the claim, (b) the insurer may recover from the insured any sums paid by the insurer to the insured in respect of the claim, and (c) in addition, the insurer may by notice to the insured treat the contract as having been terminated with effect from the time of the fraudulent act," "preserves the rule that the fraudulent claimant recovers nothing, including any unexaggerated element [but] limits the right of the insurer to avoid the whole policy to a prospective one [and] deliberately leaves open the scope of the fraudulent claims rule."

Nonetheless, the Lords in *Versloot Dredging* upheld the judgement of the Court of Appeals relying heavily on Lord Hobhouse in *Uni-Polaris*, who stated In so far as it is based upon the principle of the irrecoverability of fraudulent claims, the decision is questionable upon the facts since the actual claim made was a valid claim for a loss which had occurred and had been caused by a peril insured against when the vessel was covered by a held covered clause, [but] it is not necessary to examine whether there might or might not have been some other basis upon which the case could have been decided in favour of the insurer as one feels clearly it ought to have been [because] fraud has a fundamental impact upon the parties' relationship and raises serious public policy considerations. Remediable mistakes do not have the same character."

The foregoing is the articulation of the fraudulent claims principle which deprives the insured of the entirety of his claim should he be found guilty of fraudulent exaggeration as embodied in Insurance Act, section 12.

ADVENT OF FAIRNESS

In the case of *Mutual Energy Ltd v Starr Underwriting Agents Ltd & Anor (2016)*,[13] Justice Coulson presided over a dispute between Mutual Energy Ltd. (the "Plaintiff") a company that owns, operates and maintains an underwater link between Northern Ireland and Scotland that connects their respective electric grids called the "Moyle Interconnector," which was constructed and installed by Nexans Norway AS ("Nexans"), and two insurers (collectively, the "Defendants") who, along with three other insurers, covered the link against losses resulting from breakdowns or malfunctions. There were multiple failures between 2009 and 2011 that ultimately caused a total loss audited at tens of millions of pounds claimed by the Plaintiff and settled by three of the five insurers. The Defendants, however, sought to avoid the insurance contract ab initio refusing to compensate the Plaintiff for their share of the coverage amounting to over GBP 17 million based on the allegation of "deliberate non-disclosure" on the part of the Plaintiff pertaining to defects identified in the initial link construction and deployment faulted to Nexans but that the Plaintiff claimed were resolved prior to launch stressing the eight years of smooth operation up to the time of the claim. The Defendants allege that one or more employees of the Plaintiff were cognisant of the defects and of the fact that the information "was not being disclosed to the insurers but held the honest but mistaken belief that it need not be disclosed."

---

[13] Mutual Energy Ltd v Starr Underwriting Agents Ltd & Anor (2016)

The Defendants acknowledged that "non-disclosure or misrepresentation, negligence or breach by any one insured (or its agent) shall not be attributable to any other insured party who did not directly and actively participate in that non-disclosure or misrepresentation knowing it to be such."

The parties at trial agreed that, per sections 17 to 20 of the Marine Insurance Act, their contract was based upon the utmost good faith, every material circumstance privy to the insured must be disclosed, the insured is deemed to know every circumstances which, in the ordinary course of business, ought to be known by him on pain of contract avoidance, every circumstance is material if it would influence the insurer, and representations made during contract negotiation prior to consummation must be true. However, in their claim, the Defendants used the work "deliberate" with respect to the omission (i.e. non-disclosure) committed by the Plaintiff, and not "fraudulent." In accordance with Lord Mansfield cited above, the Defendants argued that deliberate is an "honest but mistaken decision not to disclose a document or fact in which circumstance [they] would be entitled to avoid the contract," however, they broke with tradition and accepted that if it were held that such omission was due to "indolence, inactivity or inadvertence," rather than a mistake, they would not be entitled to avoid the contract.

Justice Coulson added that, in an insurance contract such as this, there is no "dishonest wrongdoing" committed in the omission of information meaning an absence of any "element of culpability, of doing something which should not be done." But unfortunately for the Defendants, or any insurer for that matter, the ultimate effect, i.e. the deception eading to a regrettable acquiescence, is the same. "A representation may be dishonest but, f there is no intention to deceive or no intention that the misrepresentation be acted upon, then it is not fraudulent." Justice Coulson cited the Financial Ombudsman Service:[14] "It is possible to deliberately non-disclose without being fraudulent. While dishonesty is one of the essential criteria for fraud, there must also be deception, designed to obtain to which you were not entitled. [Therefore], I conclude that 'deliberate or fraudulent non-disclosure' means a deliberate decision not to disclose something which the insured knows should be disclosed, and does not extend to an honest mistake. In those circumstances, the exclusion would not be available to the insurers."

Justice Coulson went to say that the Plaintiff would "lose the benefit of the insurance if they dishonestly failed to disclose something to the [Defendants] which they should have disclosed. But they do not lose the benefit of the insurance if they considered the issue of disclosure and reached an honest but mistaken view that a particular document, or a particular fact, should not be disclosed. They are penalised for dishonesty, but not for an honest mistake. One of the things which has bedevilled the insurance industry is the ability of an insurer to avoid the contract of insurance altogether, simply because, at the time that the policy was being negotiated, the insured made a mistake and failed to disclose something which, with hindsight, he should have done." Again, this is a break with history and a sign of the emergence of something new in the adjudication of insurance claims

---

[14] Financial Ombudsman, Issue 46, May/June 2005

leaning towards "fairness" and going away with the spartan austerity and unforgiveness of the past. He considered the fact that, before the link came into operation, at least four failures were identified by Nexans and many other incidents occurred which rose serious doubts as to the integrity of the link.

Therefore, in his judgement for the Plaintiff, Justice Coulson held that although the Plaintiff was indeed aware of the potentially "poor design, manufacture, workmanship, installation and commissioning" of some of the key components of the link, this information was deliberately not disclosed before the insurance contract was concluded, and at least one employee of the Plaintiff "was aware of information and aware that it was not being disclosed to [the Defendants] but held the honest but mistaken belief that it need not be disclosed."

Therefore, the Defendants were influenced by the non-disclosures which, if the relevant information had been disclosed at the onset, they would "either have declined to write the policy at all or, if they had agreed to write it, would have done so on different terms." But in light of the new duty of fair presentation enshrined by the Insurance Act, the Plaintiff's "decision not to disclose something which was the result of an honest but mistaken belief that the fact or document did not need to be disclosed was not enough to allow the [Plaintiffs] to avoid the policy."

As one of the first cases tried under the new law, the departure from the old maxim is strikingly clear. Rather than clinging to the past, the judge was more concerned with handing down a verdict recognising that the Plaintiff had indeed presented all of its knowledge regarding the state of the link fairly and without tortious fraudulent intent and

that the Defendants could not rely on a simple error, the omission, to avoid the contract ab

initio. This is in the author's opinion the advent of fairness in the adjudication of insurance

litigation in English courts under the Insurance Act.

END

ADDENDUMS

QUESTION 1

Strict adherence to the requirement for consideration can mean that the parties' clear intentions are defeated. If it is clear that there is an agreement between two parties and that it is equally clear that they intended to be bound by their agreement, it seems unnecessary to impose a further requirement of consideration. Critically discuss.

Introduction

In the early days of English common law, *assumpsit* emerged as the dominant principle governing the interactions of the lower echelons of society based on an expressed or implied promise to undertake some obligation or perform an act in exchange for something in return.[15] Any action in court seeking recourse for a breach of assumpsit thus relied on the simple notion of quid pro quo, which later evolved into the doctrine of consideration whereby "something of value consisting of a right, interest, profit or benefit [is accrued] by one party, in exchange for a forbearance, detriment, loss or responsibility assumed by the other," as defined in *Currie v Misa*.[16]

Where a promise made in exchange for consideration moving from the promisee, or the notion of a bargain between counterparties reciprocating actions (i.e. a simple contract) is binding and the presence of consideration is necessary, a deed or so-called contract under seal executed in a way that allows an interest, right or property to exchange hands or to create a binding obligation, i.e. a specialty contract, is equally binding but the presence of

---

[15] The Free Dictionary
[16] Scribd, "Consideration and Promissory Estoppel"

consideration is unnecessary in the eyes of the court and the doctrine of promissory estoppel weighs in.[17] This is implied both in section 1 of the Law of Property[18] and section 44 of the Companies Act,[19] which lack any articulation of a requirement for reciprocity in the execution of documents embodying a clear agreement between two parties where their mutual intention to be bound thereby is equally clear, hence the doctrine of intention to create legal relations.

Therefore, the imposition of a further requirement of consideration on non-consideration based transfers of a gratuitous nature is unnecessary and may defeat the intentions of the parties, particularly in the case of *donatio inter vivos* (gifts), *donatio mortis causa* (testamentary bequeaths), and voluntary donative transfers (charitable donations), which are unsupported by consideration but binding under contract law, property law and trust & estate law, and regulated under tax law.

Promissory estoppel, an obscure facet of contract law, consists of reliance-based promises with no consideration that prevent a party to a contract from acting in a certain way because they promised not to as the other party to the contract relied on that promise and acted upon it.[20] This doctrine, along with the doctrine of intention to create legal relations, should therefore replace the doctrine of consideration in modern English law.

Gifts and Bequeaths

---

[17] In Brief, "Deeds: Contracts under seal"
[18] Law of Property (Miscellaneous Provisions) Act (1989)
[19] Companies Act (2006)
[20] Weizenbok, E., English Law of Contract: Promissory Estoppel, University of Oslo, Feb. 2012

In 1851, Sir Patrick Colquhoun[21] defined gifts according to old Roman law as *donatio inter vivos* classified as either *relata* (or *remuneratoria*), something given in exchange or reward or consideration, or *simplex* (or *absoluta*), something given "out of pure liberality without any reason being assigned or consideration." Gifts were actionable in court when accompanied by actual delivery thus constituting contracts.

Later on in Roman history, Emperor Justinian decreed gratuitous donations as *pactum legitimum* by bare consent before delivery enforceable without consideration against the donor and his heirs in favour of the prospective donee and his heirs with the sole requirement that they be expressed *per verba de præsenti*. This is over a millennium before the doctrine of estoppel found its way into English law (Colquhoun, 1851).

The flipside of the non-consideration doctrine of *donatio inter vivos* is the doctrine of *donatio mortis causa*, a gift of a testamentary nature regarded as a binding contract with no consideration whose completion is dependent solely upon the death of the donor whereby actual possession by the donee of the thing bequeathed is deferred till the death of the individual.[22] There are three requirements for these so-called deathbed gifts to be contractually complete: They must be made in contemplation of and conditional upon death, and there must be "a parting with dominion" by way of either a physical or constructive (i.e. implied) transfer or, if undeliverable due to intangibility, a delivery of

---

[21] Colquhoun, P., Summary of Roman Civil Law, ss.1058 & 1059, William Benning & Co., London, 1851
[22] Moffett, W., Deathbed gifts in rude health: the recent case of Vallée v Birchwood, Radcliffe Chambers, 2013

"indicia of title" is required, as established in *Birch v Treasury Solicitor*, which is articulated as "deeds" in the Law of Property Act (Moffett, 2013).

Fry LJ in 1890 ruled on a case regarding a donated horse stating that "where a gift of a chattel capable of delivery is made *per verba de præsenti* by a donor to a donee, and is assented to by the donee, and that assent is communicated to the donor by the donee, there is a perfect gift which passes the property without delivery of the chattel itself."[23] His Lordship and the Roman Emperor Justinian were thus in harmony with regard to perfecting non-consideration based gifts.

This was partially echoed in *Trustee v Cole* (1964)[24] with the exclusion of delivery as a requirement. This precedential case in English property law involved a bankrupt man's wife seeking the return of chattels (specifically, the contents of a home) that had been seized by creditors based on her claim that they were gifted to her prior to his bankruptcy and therefore separate from his estate.

Harman LJ, ruling against the wife, held that a gift is complete when there is intention, actual delivery (i.e. change of possession), and acceptance. Only one requirement was present in this case, that of donor intent, and his Lordship resurrected the requirement of delivery for gift perfection set forth by Fry LJ three-quarters of a century earlier, mirroring pre-Justinian Roman law.

---

[23] IUS Commune Casebooks for the Common Law of Europe, section 8.7, Court of Appeal, Queens Bench Division, 28 Apr. 1890
[24] Re Cole (1964)

Generally, therefore, *inter vivos* gifts must be accompanied by donative intent and delivery on the part of the donor, and acceptance on the part of the donee. If any of these are not present, then the gift fails, and there is zero requirement to uphold the doctrine of consideration.

Estoppel

Promissory estoppel is essentially an equitable doctrine based on fairness not supported by consideration which works to stop a person going back on a promise.[25] There must be (1) a pre-existing legal relationship between the parties, (2) a clear and unambiguous promise or representation, either expressed or implied, that one party will not insist on their strict legal rights against the other, with the promisor intending to affect the legal relationship between the parties, and (3) any change in the position in reliance on that promise or representation would be unfair to the promisee (Franklins, 2016).

Without any reference to the doctrine of consideration, the idea underlying the doctrine of promissory estoppel consists of stopping someone from going back on a representation intended to induce someone to rely thereon.[26] It only applies to prevent someone from going back on a promise that they have made not to enforce some legal right that they have against someone else. One cannot waive a right with respect to another resulting in the latter's reliance on that promise, and subsequently enforce that right, i.e. going back on the

[25] Franklins Solicitors LLP, "Moore v Moore," 9 Dec. 2016
[26] McBrides Guides, "The law on estoppel," 8 Sept. 2012

original promise to waive it. This principle was first articulated by Lord Cairns LC in *Hughes v Metropolitan Railway* (1877), as follows:

"[If the parties to a contract] enter upon a course of negotiation which has the effect of leading one of the parties to suppose that the strict rights arising under the contract will not be enforced, or will be kept in suspense, or held in abeyance, the person who otherwise might have enforced those rights will not be allowed to enforce them where it would be inequitable having regard to the dealings between those parties."

The doctrine has the effect of making some kinds of promises binding even where they are not supported by consideration. The absence of consideration does not mean no contract, it means no enforceable contract, and this becomes clear when comparing gift promises that are enforced, gift promises that are not enforced, and the use of promissory estoppel to enforce promises admittedly lacking consideration (Weizenbok, 2012).

Denning J in Central London Property Trust v High Trees (1947)[27] stated that "[There] are cases of promises which were intended to create legal relations and which, in the knowledge of the person making the promise, were going to be acted on by the party to whom the promise was made, and have in fact been so acted on. In such cases the courts have said [each] promise must be honoured and [binding] on the party making it…notwithstanding the absence of consideration.

---

[27] Central London Property Trust, Ltd. v High Trees House, Ltd. (1947)

"[In] the sixth interim report of the Law Revision Committee, it was recommended that such a promise...should be enforceable in law even though no consideration had been given by the promisee."

His Lordship, therefore, held that a prima facie promise is binding and, based on the recommendations of the Law Revision Committee,[28] partially outlined below, set aside the doctrine of consideration as a relic of old common law in favour of promissory estoppel and intention to create legal relations.

Setting Aside Consideration

On the question of consideration, the Law Revision Committee, in its Sixth Interim Report published in 1937 (hereinafter, "the Report"), duly cited by Lord Denning as per the foregoing, points to the "the serious inconveniences which arise from the doctrine and the rules which have grown up around it." Since its application neither distinguishes between onerous and gratuitous contracts, nor sets aside arrangements with no legal consequences, it cannot be justified. "It breeds technicality in the shape of nominal consideration, and is of so uncompromising a character that departures have been necessary in the interest of elementary justice which cannot be defended on grounds of logic (e.g. past consideration given at the request of the promisor may support a subsequent promise)."

The Report describes strict adherence to the doctrine of consideration as (1) defeating the intention of the parties, (2) permitting the most cynical disregard of promises solemnly

---

[28] The Modern Law Review, Vol. 1, No. 2, Sixth Interim Report, The Law Revision Committee, Sept. 1937, pp.4-11

undertaken, (3) responsible for hardship and inconvenience where it establishes that a gratuitous promise to keep an offer open is not binding, (4) a mere technicality irreconcilable either with business expediency or common sense, and (5) frequently provides loopholes for escape from a promise deliberately given with intent to create a binding obligation and in reliance thereon the promisee may have acted.

Proffered therein are recommendations to alleviate and mitigate the negative outcomes heretofore engendered by strict juridical adherence to the doctrine of consideration. The very first on the list is its abolishment "root and branch" or, if deemed too extreme a remedy, the indoctrination of present and past consideration as equal in value and elevation of writing (i.e. deeds and contracts under seal) to the status of consideration in English law.

Another interesting recommendation is the abolishment of the Rule in Pinnel's Case as "one of the most absurd doctrines which have succeeded in becoming established as part of the English law of contract...based upon a confusion between consideration and satisfaction."

Mutual promises are defined in the Report as consideration bestowed on each other, where giving consideration in an agreement by one counterparty in the form of a promise to the other already bound by law to perform an act or fulfil a promise is in and of itself consideration. A promise begetting consideration as a natural outcome begets a counter-promise with more consideration and so on, thus rendering consideration as a doctrine both obsolete and unnecessary since the equitable doctrine of estoppel can serve just as well and respects the true intentions of the counterparties.

The Report provides a scathing critique of one of the oldest doctrines in English law for which a solution was finally espoused half a century later by Russel LJ in *Williams v Roffey Bros* (1989) advocating the replacement of consideration altogether with the doctrine of intention to create legal relations. [29] Combining legal intent with estoppel, therefore, sufficiently binds counterparties without bowing to the archaic notions of our ancestors e.g. the arbitrary determination of sufficient or nominal consideration; The Law Revision Committee, 1937).

On a side note, Lord Mansfield ruled in 1765 that credit confirmed by a bank or merchant (i.e. the promise to accept drafts) was enforceable without consideration. This attack on the doctrine was later upheld and affirmed in the House of Lords, ushering in an entire industry with international implications. His Lordship was not successful, however, later on when he advocated the interpretation of land transfers based on "plain intention."[30]

Conclusion

The strict adherence to the doctrine of consideration may, as demonstrated above, be troublesome and could very well be replaced by the combination of the doctrines of intention to create legal relations and promissory estoppel. They intertwine in two specific precedential cases, namely Kleinwort Benson v Malaysia Mining Corporation (1989)[31] and *Errington v Errington Woods* (1952).[32] The former involves a bank bringing an action in court

---

[29] Tutor Hunt website, "Should Consideration be Abolished?", 21 Oct. 2013
[30] Llewellyn, K., "William Murray, 1st Earl of Mansfield," Encyclopædia Britannica, 13 Mar. 2018
[31] Kleinwort Benson, Ltd. v Malaysia Mining Corp BHD
[32] Errington v Errinton and Another

against an insolvent mining concern claiming that a letter of comfort issued by its parent entity, which did not guarantee the loan in question, constituted a promise to ensure its subsidiary's sound financial position enforceable under the estoppel doctrine and relied upon as assurance. Gibson LJ held that the said letter was in effect a non-binding articulation of parent entity policy, and its refusal to act as guarantor demonstrated a lack of intention to create legal relations. His Lordship ruled in favour of the defendant with little mention of consideration which, quoting Lord Hirst, does not serve to bind an agreement in absence of the intent to create legal relations.

In *Errington*, the father's promise to give a house to his son and daughter-in-law as wedding gift was challenged in court by his widow, the mother, who inherited the house after her husband's untimely death as it had been unfortunately placed in his name alone. In response to the late father's promise, the young couple had promised to pay the mortgage, which they continued to do so even after relations with the mother had soured. Lord Denning held that the father's promise stood as an expression of intent to create legal relations and the mother was estopped from revoking it because acceptance had already taken place and performance, i.e. the actual fulfilment of the counter-promise of the couple to make payments on the house, had already commenced. This was a challenge to the doctrine of consideration with respect to family and social engagements, or the tendency in English law to view familial or friendly dealings and affairs as non-binding.

Therefore, as demonstrated in these cases, strict adherence to the requirement for consideration can defeat the parties' clear intentions and, if an agreement between two arties clearly exists and their intention to be bound by their agreement is equally clear, it

s unnecessary to impose a further requirement of consideration, whose doctrine can be

eplaced with that of promissory estoppel and intention to create legal relations.

QUESTION 2

Consider whether the criminal law now has the right balance when dealing with defendants who have committed the actus reus of an offence but may have reduced or no culpability for their actions.

Introduction

Any attempt to properly examine the imbalance in the English criminal justice system with respect to how defendants who actually committed offences are determined as having diminished or lacking criminal responsibility as a result of successfully pleading insanity or automatism begins with the M'Naghten Rules established by the House of Lords in 1843, which states that "to establish a defence on the ground of insanity, it must be clearly proved that, at the time of the committing of the act, the party accused was labouring under such a defect of reason, from disease of the mind as not to know the nature and quality of the act he was doing, or if he did know it, that he did not know he was doing what was wrong."[33] The imbalance lies in the fundamentally unjust notion of inculpability due to lack of sufficient reason to assume responsibility resulting from some 'disease of the mind' either chronic or contemporaneously realized at the precise moment of the crime which eliminated either the cognisance of the act or omission by effectively removing subjective reasoning, or the understanding of it as "wrong," i.e. "contrary to law" per *R v Windle (1952)*,[34] having established that the perpetrator was mindful of the act. At issue here is the

---

[33] M'Naghten Rules
[34] R v Windle (1952)

mental health of the criminal or his mental state at the time or in the course of the act or series of acts or omission that constituted the actus reus and (1) whether criminal responsibility should be reduced or waived for those who successfully prove to the satisfaction of the court that their ability to reason and understand the nature of their acts was deficient due to insanity, i.e. diminished capacity caused by a strictly internal factor, or automatism, i.e. the body acting independently of conscious thought or intention triggered by an internal or external factor resulting from a physical or mental condition, ailment or dysfunction beyond the control of the offender such as somnambulism, schizophrenia, or syncope stemming from hypoglycaemia, inebriation or anxiety, or contrastingly, (2) whether it is morally justifiable to convict the mentally ill or those prone to automatism for criminal acts they had no control over due to lack of mens rea committed through no fault of their own.[35]

The Insanity Plea

Any defendant pleading insanity for a crime he has been proven to have committed is obligated to manoeuvre his defence within the parameters set out by *M'Naghten*. If the Court is satisfied beyond a reasonable doubt, the "special verdict" of not guilty by reason of insanity is handed down and the defendant is either fully discharged, placed under the supervision of a social worker or probation officer, or detained at a mental health treatment facility until deemed fit to be released back into society as determined at the discretion of

---

[35] Law Commission, *Criminal Liability: Insanity and Automatism*, (Law Com No 311, 2008) para 1.18-19

the Prosecutors according to the defendant's condition, per section 5 of the Criminal Procedure (Insanity) Act 1964.[36,37] These broad disposal powers are available only to the Crown Court, which must "consider whether a prosecution is even required if the suspect [suffers] from any significant mental or physical ill health[,] whether [the offence] is likely to be repeated and the need to safeguard the public or those providing care [thereto]."[38] So the criminal justice system grinds to a halt and judges waive their duty to administer justice whenever a defendant provides corroborable evidence of mental or physical illness? The Magistrates' Court, however, which only tries summary offences, i.e. minor charges with no right to a jury, can only dispose of a mentally ill defendant in such ways if duly convicted of his crime, i.e. found criminally responsible. Contrastingly, if a mentally ill perpetrator of even a minor, victimless crime such as stalking or petty theft, for example, is acquitted by reason of insanity by the Magistrates' Court, its only disposal option is absolute discharge to the detriment of society. No mandatory treatment or monitoring. Another discrepancy is mens rea. The Magistrates' Court requires that mens rea be proven for insanity to be entered as a defence, meaning that one cannot plead insanity without a provable mental element, and there is no preliminary procedure available to assess a mentally ill individual's fitness to stand trial or render a plea.[39]

---

[36] Ibid para 1.25
[37] Criminal Procedure (Insanity) Act
[38] The Code for Crown Prosecutors, 7th Edition, January 2013
[39] Law Commission, *Criminal Liability: Insanity and Automatism*, (Law Com No 311, 2008) para 1.13, 1.54, 1.55, 1.121

he Crown Court, meanwhile, only requires that the actus reus be proven as having resulted rom mental illness-begotten diminished capacity per *M'Naghten*, and an insanity plea can ie entered freely irrespective of whether the offence in question contained a mental element, e.g. motoring offences, mayhem, recklessness, negligence, possession, etc. If ound not guilty by reason of insanity in the Magistrates' Court, the verdict is complete icquittal. Not so at the Crown Court, whose special verdict established in section 2(1) of Trial of Lunatics Act 1883 [40] triggers the foregoing selection of humane and socially ieneficial disposals. A mentally ill offender acquitted by the Magistrates' Court for reason of insanity is not handed a special verdict and referred to the Crown Court for disposal with any aim of ameliorating his condition through treatment or guidance, nor of protecting :hose directly involved or society.[41]

There are also cases where statutes clash and defendants are jockeyed between the hallowed institutions of the judicial system. In the European Court of Human Rights case of *Antoine v. United Kingdom (2003)*,[42] the applicant, a paranoid schizophrenic convicted of accessory to murder in a satanic ritual, initially entered a guilty plea to manslaughter by reason of diminished responsibility that was accepted by the Crown. Counsel submitted that the applicant was unfit to plead or to stand trial by reason of mental disorder and the trial judge directed the jury as such in accordance with *R v. Pritchard*[43] (1836; Fitness to

---

[40] Trial of Lunatics Act 1883
[41] Law Commission, *Insanity and Automatism: Supplementary Material to the Scoping Paper* (2012) para 2.9
[42] Antoine v. United Kingdom (2003)
[43] R v. Pritchard (1836)

plead: "The applicant is unable to instruct his legal representatives to plead to the indictment, to challenge jurors, or to understand the evidence or to give evidence in his own defence"). Based on medical reports brought into evidence, he was committed to a mental asylum subject to restriction without limitation per the provisions of Part III of the Mental Health Act 1983.[44] Per section 4A of the Criminal Procedure (Insanity) Act 1964, a second jury was empanelled in order to determine whether the applicant did in fact commit the actus reus. In this so-called "section 4A hearing," the defendant attempted to plead diminished responsibility, but the trial judge refused and took the unusual step of requiring that the prosecution prove both the actus reus as well as the mens rea. The Court of Appeal later upheld the decision but questioned whether a person found unfit to plead AND then tried for murder under section 4A could even be allowed to plead diminished responsibility. The House of Lords later reaffirmed that only the actus reus had to be proven in a section 4A hearing and that mens rea is only relevant in case of a "mistake, accident or self-defence with no possibility of submitting the statutory defence of diminished responsibility," which is only available when charged with murder under section 2 of the Homicide Act 1957.[45] Therefore, if determined as unfit to plead, the trial is suspended and a murder conviction is no longer an option despite the fact that he indeed, without a shred of doubt, committed the actus reus per the conclusions of the section 4A hearing. That individual then cleverly beseeched the European Court of Human Rights to determine whether his human rights as

---

[44] Mental Health Act 1983
[45] Homicide Act 1957

efined by the European Charter of Human Rights had been violated under Article 3

nhuman or degrading treatment or punishment), Article 5 (arbitrary detention) and Article

(right to a fair trial and presumption of innocence). His case was thrown out as baseless.

roffering the leading judgment in *Antoine*, Lord Hutton stated shockingly that the

efendant, due to his insanity at the time of the commission of the offence, had in fact

done nothing wrong" and the "injurious act would constitute a crime only if done with the

equisite mens rea."

he Automatism Plea

he common law defence of automatism may be entered into the court record by any

efendant for any crime and, if sufficient evidence is presented, the Prosecution is required

o disprove it to secure a conviction. Failure on their part results in an outright acquittal

ith no special verdict as for insanity pleas.[46] Where insanity is defined as unintentional,

nvoluntary acts caused by an internal factor, i.e. mental, psychological, psychiatric, etc.,

vhose perpetrator is graciously bestowed the special verdict, or not guilty by reason of

nsanity, automatism constitutes acts spurred by some specific external factor such as

eflex, intoxication, stress disorders or sleep deprivation, known as "sane automatism", or

n internal factor such as diabetic and epileptic comas, hypoglycaemic blackouts, etc.,

nown as "insane automatism," which generally lead to acquittals if satisfactorily

demonstrated. [47] Precedential cases involving automatism range from the downright

---

[46] Law Commission, *Criminal Liability: Insanity and Automatism, (Law Com No 311, 2008) para 1.27-28*
[47] *Ibid para 1.41*

comical to the morbidly sobering. In *R v Wholley*, a truck driver sneezed several times in a fit and momentarily lost control of his vehicle causing a chain reaction that smashed 7 cars on the highway. His plea of involuntary action by sane automatism was successful, as the Magistrates' Court acquitted him and the Court of Appeal upheld the verdict.[48] In my view he should have had the good sense to apply the breaks immediately at the first sneeze. The Merriam Webster Dictionary defines sneezing as "a sudden violent spasmodic audible expiration of breath through the nose and mouth especially as a reflex act." How can this ever result in momentary diminished capacity or reason depriving him of cognisance of his acts?

Contrastingly, the automatism case of *R. v Sullivan (1984)* is no laughing matter. In this case, grievous bodily harm was inflicted on a man by Mr. Sullivan during a lengthy lapse of consciousness and memory in the wake of an epileptic seizure. Medical evidence was insufficient to convince the presiding judge, who labelled the act as insanity and handed down the special verdict, which if upheld would have resulted in the remanding of Mr. Sullivan to a mental asylum. As he clearly was not insane, he wanted to avoid being labelled as such at all costs and luckily was permitted to change his plea after the ruling from involuntary action by automatism to assault, for which he was convicted. Even though this conviction was by far better than a prolonged stint in the looney farm, Mr. Sullivan

---

[48] InBrief, "Automatism as a Criminal Defence"

onetheless attempted to get it overturned at the Court of Appeal, to no avail, then the ouse of Lords, which turned him away upholding the original judgement.

he imbalance that the learned judges hearing his appeals inadvertently created in their eemingly concerted effort to avoid the special verdict is their expressed labelling as utright insanity the psychological state immediately following an epileptic seizure, whilst orrectly questioning the legality and propriety of allowing the defendant to change his plea fter the verdict had been cast.[49]

ord Diplock, in my view, erred in stating in his judgement for this case that, when scertaining a 'disease of the mind' per *M'Naghten* as a factor in the commission of a crime, it matters not whether the aetiology of the impairment is organic, as in epilepsy, or unctional, or whether the impairment itself is permanent or is transient and intermittent, rovided that it subsisted at the time of commission of the act," thus equating any nvoluntary act resulting from an internal factor like epilepsy as insanity plain and simple. :learly there is discord at the highest levels of the judicial system with regard to medical cience and the effects or repercussions that certain physical conditions and ailments may 1ave on perfectly sane minds.

:onclusion

3ased on the foregoing, there is an evident imbalance in the UK criminal justice system with ·egard to properly administering justice on behalf of the victims of at times gruesome

⁹ Lederman, E., Non-Insane and Insane Automatism: Reducing the Significant of a Problematic Distinction, *nternational & Comparative Law Quarterly*, Online, Cambridge University Press, 4 October 1985, Volume 34, Issue 4, pp. 819-837

crimes perpetrated at the hands of the persistently, chronically or temporarily insane. This imbalance is engendered by (1) the archaic tenets and rules used as the basis for ascertaining the role of complex mental health conditions in the commissioning of crimes, (2) multiple and at times conflicting legislation on the books, namely the Trial of Lunatics Act 1883, the Homicide Act of 1957, Criminal Procedure (Insanity) Act 1964 and the Mental Health Act 1983, (3) the availability of certain disposals at some courts but not at others, and (4) the tendency of certain judges to sometimes label involuntary acts as insane demonstrating a blatant incomprehension of the effects that certain physical ailments or dysfunctions have on consciousness or awareness. What indelibly results are murderers found innocent under the law due to the absence of mens rea who are committed to comfortable modern medical facilities for psychiatric evaluation and treatment and released upon confirmation of improvement in their conditions, in addition to confusion and discrepancies in court proceedings at all levels that lead to costly appeals and time wasted, as well as perfectly sane persons found not criminally responsible for the crimes they in fact committed thanks to automatism-triggered momentary diminished capacity and set free untethered and untreated.

QUESTION 3

Discuss the following statement: Modern approach to statutory interpretation requires the judges to move towards the purposive method of interpretation. Criteria: Outline the methods of judicial interpretation with references to the case law examples. Discuss the transition of judicial approach towards the statutory interpretation and its impact on English Legal System.

Statutory Interpretation, a Brief History

The weaving of Parliamentary statutes into the fabric of judicial precedent through their interpretation and application by judges presiding over cases throughout England's history has its roots centuries ago when the legislature's role and authority were broadened and enhanced to legitimise the rule of the Sovereign and attain other historical intentions.[50]

The Tudors, King James I and Oliver Cromwell alike wielded Parliament as a device to solidify their power, and its promulgated laws thus came to be regarded as sovereign and supreme in themselves, and treated by English courts as having special binding force (Sales LJ). From as early as the Elizabethan Age through to the present day, judges have interpreted statutes relevant to the cases they were presiding over in accordance with either the "literal rule," which consists of a strict adherence to the exact meaning of the wording contained therein precisely due to the foregoing reason (Sales LJ), or the "golden rule" or "mischief rule," which are manifestations of a judge's prerogative to sensibly interpret a statute based on

---

[50] Lord Justice Philip Sales, Modern Statutory Interpretation, Statute Law Society

Parliament's intention whenever the application of its literal sense would be absurd, or any ambiguity would require further development, evolution, or adaptation by the judge in the ruling.[51] These constitute the "domestic rules" of which the literal rule must always be applied first, followed by either one of the other two in an attempt to remedy whatever shortcomings the literal sense of a statute's wording may have when applied verbatim.[52] Gradually, rather than simply apply the "bald meaning" of the language in a statute, judges began to consider the purpose of the law interpreting it flexibly to ensure justice and fairness, factoring in the background and presumptions of the case at hand and respecting basic constitutional values (Sales LJ).

The conventional practice of basing judicial rulings on common law with reference to statutes duly interpreted to supplement precedent, albeit with occasional discretionary fine-tuning of either preposterousness or vagueness, evolved into a positivist approach commencing in the late 19th Century, which predates the modern purposive approach that permeated Europe in the late 20th Century with its wider, inclusive aim and consideration for human and constitutional rights, fairness, due process and other implications (Sales LJ). The following is a chronological synopsis of the development of judicial statutory interpretation by English courts from the Victorian Age up to the modern requirement of judges to apply the European purposive approach.

Remedying Mischief at Sea

---

[51] E-Law Resources
[52] Ibid.

he mischief rule was applied in *Gorris v Scott* (1874), a claim for indemnification for the ss of sheep at sea washed overboard from the defendant's ship.[53] The plaintiff claimed at the defendant did not comply with the Contagious Diseases Act (1864), which requires e shipowner to have separate dens for the animals on the ship[54] in an effort to minimise e spread of contagious diseases by restricting the movement of animals and their contact ith each other. The claim is for the loss of the sheep due to drowning, not disease, and usly did not correspond to the particular mischief that Parliament attempted to remedy ith the Act, which is "directed against the possibility of sheep or cattle being exposed to isease on their way to this country." The judges ruled against the plaintiff as oncompliance of the statute on the part of the defendant resulted in a harm that the Act as never designed to protect against.

n hindsight, perhaps Lloyd's of London could have insured them or, instead of a law oncerned mainly with venereal diseases in Victorian society, the plaintiff could have rought the case for judgement to the High Court of Admiralty based on section 6 of the dmiralty Court Act (1861; "The High Court of Admiralty shall have jurisdiction over any laim by the owner or consignee or assignee of any bill of lading of any goods carried into ny port in England or Wales in any ship for damage done to the goods or any part thereof y the negligence or misconduct of or for any breach of duty or breach of contract on the

---

[3] Law Mentor

[4] 4LawSchool

part of the owner, master or crew of the ship")[55], whereby the word "goods" would have likely been interpreted to include livestock and Mr. Gorris would have been provided due compensation for his loss.

Remedying Absurdity for Trespassers and Murderers

Lord Wensleydale in *Grey v Pearson* (1857) defined the golden rule of statutory interpretation by instructing that "the grammatical and ordinary sense of the words is to be adhered to unless that would lead to some absurdity or some repugnance or inconsistency...in which case [they] may be modified so as to avoid the absurdity and inconsistency, but no farther."[56]

In *Adler v George* (1964), the words "the vicinity of" in section 3 of the Official Secrets Act (1920; "No person in the vicinity of any prohibited place shall obstruct, knowingly mislead or otherwise interfere with or impede, the chief officer or a superintendent or other officer of police, or any member of His Majesty's forces")[57] were interestingly the focus of the case involving the arrest of the plaintiff at Markham Royal Air Force Station, Norfolk, for trespassing and obstruction. He claimed that since he was actually "in" that prohibited military base at the time of his arrest, and therefore not "in the vicinity of" the same, then the charge should be revoked. Since the literal rule would have obviously resulted in an absurd ruling, the court used the golden rule to interpret the statute in a way so that it could

---

[55] Admiralty Court Act (1861)
[56] Grey v Pearson (1857)
[57] Official Secrets Act (1920), section 3

pply in his case, as "someone protesting near the base would be committing an offence

whilst someone protesting in it would not.[58]

he *Sigsworth* (1935) case involved the murder of a woman by her son who, despite his

einous crime, would have inherited her estate as next of kin due to the lack of a last will

nd testament in accordance with section 1 of the Administration of Estates Act (1925; (1)

eal estate to which a deceased person was entitled for an interest not ceasing on his death

hall on his death, and notwithstanding any testamentary disposition thereof, devolve from

ime to time on the personal representative of the deceased, in like manner as before the

ommencement of this Act chattels real devolved on the personal representative from time

o time of a deceased person, (2) The personal representatives for the time being of a

deceased person are deemed in law his heirs and assigns within the meaning of all trusts

nd powers).[59]

Whilst the statute was clearly free of ambiguity and absurdity, its literal interpretation

would have forced the court to hand over the estate to that murderer allowing him to

benefit from his crime. The golden rule was thus applied "to prevent the repugnant

situation of the son inheriting" by Judge Clauson who held that "the principle of public policy

which precludes a murderer from claiming a benefit conferred on him by his victim's will

precludes him from claiming a benefit conferred on him, in a case of his victim's intestacy,

by statute.[60]

---

[58] The Open University, 6.3 "The Golden Rule"
[59] Administration of Estates Act (1925)
[60] Swarb website, Re Sigsworth: Bedford v Bedford (1935)

Positivism, the Precursor of Modern Statutory Interpretation

An example of the positivist approach to statutory interpretation, the precursor of the modern purposive approach, is the ruling in *Ridge v Baldwin* (1964),[61] a case involving an administrative decision by the Brighton police authority (the "Watch Committee") to fire its Chief Constable that was appealed to the House of Lords as "void and of no effect because he had no notice of the grounds on which the Committee proposed to act and no opportunity to be heard in his own defence" by the Appellant. The power of dismissal vested in an English police authority with respect to its constables is articulated in section 191 (4) of the Municipal Corporations Act (1882), which states that such authority "may at any time suspend...or dismiss any borough constable whom they think negligent in the discharge of his duty, or otherwise unfit for the same."[62]

Had the Lords simply applied the literal rule to the interpretation of this statute, they would have held in favour of the Respondent. However, the principles of *audi alteram partem* ("hear both sides") and due process, the foundation of natural justice, were clearly not upheld in their resolution to fire Chief Constable Ridge, a knee-jerk reaction after his corruption indictment subsequently thrown out due to lack of evidence, thus opening the door to the application of the positivist approach of the Lords in their ruling against them. Failure to inform him of the charges and to provide him with a fair opportunity to defend himself before a decision was reached by the competent authority is a violation of the

---

[61] Arbitration, Practice & Procedure Law Reports
[62] Municipal Corporations Act (1882)

principle of natural justice (Lord Reid). Despite the letter of the applicable law, which neither made mention to due process nor outlined a procedure for the actual dismissal, the court saw fit to apply the universal principal of fairness.

Human Rights and Statutory Interpretation

An example of how statutory interpretation evolved in the early 21st Century in England into the modern purposive approach is demonstrated in the opposite way that similar legislation regarding the succession of tenancy due to death was interpreted by judges in two separate cases, namely *Harrogate Borough Council v Simpson* (1985) and *Ghaidan v Godin-Mendoza* (2004), which occurred before and after the promulgation of the Human Rights Act (1998),[63] whose Section 3 (1) requires judges to "read and given effect [to legislation] in a way which is compatible with the Convention rights,"[64] i.e. Articles 1 and 14 of the European Convention on Human Rights (1953)[65] regarding the prohibition of gender-based discrimination.

The controversial statutes in question are paragraph 2 of Schedule 1 of the Rent Act (1977): "If the original tenant was a man who died leaving a widow who was residing with him at his death then, after his death, the widow shall be the statutory tenant if and so long as she occupies the dwelling-house as her residence,"[66] and section 30 (2) of the Housing Act 1980): "A person is qualified to succeed the tenant under a secure tenancy if he occupied

---

[63] Pearson Education Catalogue
[64] Human Rights Act (1998)
[65] European Convention on Human Rights (1953)
[66] Rent Act (1977)

the dwelling-house as his only or principal home at the time of the tenant's death and [is the tenant's spouse."[67] In the latter, a spouse is defined as someone living "together as husband and wife." These citations are from the original texts of the statutes subsequentl altered once after the revised Housing Act (1988) and then again after the Civil Partnershi Act (2004) were adopted.

In the *Simpson* case, the claimant had lived with the deceased, the "secure tenant," in lesbian relationship for some years and was so living at the date of her death, an importan criterion of tenancy succession. She sought to defend her occupation asserting that she qualified as the spouse of the deceased. In his ruling, Judge Ewbank stated that "the expression 'living together as husband and wife' is not apt to include a homosexua relationship. The essential characteristic of living together as husband and wife, in my judgment, is that there should be a man and a woman."[68] The literal rule was thus applie to deny Ms. Simpson the succession of the tenancy of the dwelling based on the exact meaning of the words "husband and wife."

Contrastingly, in the *Ghaidan* case[69] brought before the House of Lords on appeal well after passage of the Human Rights Act, the secure tenant, Mr. Wallwyn-James, died and the landlord brought proceedings in court claiming possession of the dwelling. The presiding judge, after having denied Mr. Godin-Mendoza, the long-time same-sex partner who shared the dwelling with Mr. Wallwyn-James for many years, statutory tenancy as the legitimate

---

[67] Housing Act (1980)
[68] Harrogate Borough Council v Simpson (1985)
[69] Ghaidan v. Godin-Mendoza (2004)

ccessor under the 2(2) of Schedule 1 of the Rent Act (1977), nonetheless held that he "did ecome entitled to an 'assured' tenancy...by succession as a member of the original tenant's amily' under paragraph 3(1)" of the said Act thus sparking the dissatisfied landlord's appeal o the House of Lords. The difference between an assured tenancy and a secure, or tatutory, tenancy are subtle on the surface but the contractual terms and conditions of the ease are more advantageous to the landlord both monetarily and in terms of control over he property. An assured tenant may be charged more rent than a secure tenant, and the ormer's eviction and possession order are easier to obtain. Recognising the landlord's motive, the presiding judge held that "in these and some other respects the succession ights granted by the statute to the survivor of a homosexual couple in respect of the house where he or she is living are less favourable than the succession rights granted to the urvivor of a heterosexual couple" (Lord Nicholls), and thus discriminatory and a violation f Convention rights.

he lower court judge had applied a combination of the literal rule and purposive approach o statutory interpretation in his ruling asserting a clear distinction between the survivor of a heterosexual couple having the right of statutory tenancy by succession (i.e. the literal meaning of "husband" or "wife"), and the survivor of a homosexual couple who, while duly recognised as the significant other of the departed individual, was arbitrarily subordinated to the rank of "family" entitling him to assured tenancy, and in doing so only partially affording him the human rights guaranteed under the Convention.

"Mr. Godin-Mendoza's claim is that this difference in treatment infringes article 14 of the European Convention on Human Rights read in conjunction with article 8. But if the state makes legislative provision it must not be discriminatory. The provision must not draw a distinction on grounds such as sex or sexual orientation without good reason. Unless justified, a distinction founded on such grounds infringes the Convention right embodied in article 14, as read with article 8. Mr. Godin-Mendoza submits that the distinction drawn by paragraph 2 of Schedule 1 to the Rent Act 1977 is drawn on the grounds of sexual orientation and that this difference in treatment lacks justification. Hence he is entitled to a declaration that on the death of Mr Wallwyn-James he succeeded to a statutory tenancy." (Lord Nicholls) This is a great leap forward compared to *Simpson* exemplifying our ability to apply universal principles to statutes intentionally articulated for narrow purposes with the broader, more inclusive aim of building a vast liberal democratic society across Europe where fundamental rights are upheld and legal certainty is ensured.

Conclusion

Whilst the multiple languages of Community legislation interpreted by the European Court of Justice preclude the application of the literal rule, its purposive approach going beyond its wording and considering its general aim from the perspective of the wider community of Member States as a whole, permeated into English courts in the late 20th Century engendering a new kind of legal certainty. Judges are now required to look past standard dictionary definitions of the words contained in statutes and consider human rights, irness, due process, and other implications in their interpretation with the entire EU in

ind.

he evolution of statutory interpretation spans from obstinate observance of the binding,

overeign letter of the law, to creative flexibilities afforded to remedy injustices, and finally

the modern purposive approach that emerged as a consequence to the application of

ommunity legislation and enshrinement of constitutional rights.

QUESTION 4

Discuss how the EU has developed the principle of recognition of professional qualification

in the protection of freedom of establishment.

Introduction and Intent of the Framers

The principle of recognition of professional qualifications has its roots in Article 47 of the

Treaty of Rome (1957), which later became Article 53 of the Treaty on the Functioning of

the European Union (2007; hereinafter, "the Treaty"), as follows: "In order to make it easier

for persons to take up and pursue activities as self-employed persons, the European

Parliament and the Council shall, acting in accordance with the ordinary legislative

procedure, issue directives for the mutual recognition of diplomas, certificates and other

evidence of formal qualifications and for the coordination of the provisions laid down by

law, regulation or administrative action in Member States concerning the taking-up and

pursuit of activities as self-employed persons."[70]

What did the framers of the Treaty have in mind when they applied the broad strokes in the

conceptualisation of this principle? Did they realise that an arduous road lay ahead towards

full and comprehensive enfranchisement? The following is a brief summarisation of the

development of mutual recognition of professional qualifications from the early years of

the EEC and its initial Directives focused on specific vocations, through to 2013, the year the

fully-modernised and comprehensive Professional Qualifications Directive was adopted.

---

[70] Treaty on the Functioning of the European Union (2007)

1e first phase, spanning from the early 1960s through to the mid-70s, in the development
′ the principle of recognition of professional qualifications in the EEC is categorised by a
ansitional approach (Kortese, p.5) with respect to occupations in commerce, industry, and
afts.[71] Some of the measures implemented during that era granted the recognition of
revious work experience for self-employed persons specifically engaged in manufacturing
1d processing. Directive 64/429, for example, abolished restrictions on certain activities
assified in the Nomenclature of Industries in the European Communities, a list initially
⊃mpiled in 1961, paving the way for skilled labour mobility and the attainment of the
eedom of provision of services and establishment.[72]

While striking a positive note, an objective reading of this Directive clearly demonstrates
rotectionism for specific domestic industries and activities (Article 3). It also set forth
⊃ecific alien identification registration requirements in certain host countries (Article 4-2,
to E) and obligates foreigners to produce evidence of, or swear an oath to, their "good
epute" and solvency, i.e. lack of bankruptcy history (Article 7, 1 and 2). Other Directives of
1at era dealt with retail, the so-called "personal services," i.e. restaurants, taverns, hotels
nd the like, and targeted self-employed persons and intermediaries, or brokers, engaged

---

′ Kortese, L., "Exploring professional recognition in the EU: a legal perspective," Journal of international
Mobility, 2016/1 (N° 4), p. 43-58
′ Directive 64/429/EEC

in the trade, distribution and professional usage of coal and toxic products. Later on insurance, transportation and travel agents were added.[73]

The focus was clearly to promote the mobility of blemish-free, autonomous, well-financed qualified (albeit low-tech), small-scale tradesmen, salesmen and industrialists capable of relocating to a more promising area of the EEC and setting up shop. Perhaps legislators envisioned such enterprising sole-proprietors hiring many of the millions of economic migrants who ventured out to the EEC in search of a better life during the 1960s. Over 8 million foreign labourers were granted work permits over the decade and a half period between the signing of the Treaty of Rome and the OPEC oil crisis of 1973.[74]

While promising and forward-looking, legislators limited their scope during this crucial period when the right of freedom of establishment was in its infancy, reserving enfranchisement to a select few.

Sectoral Directives and the Plight of Migrant Lawyers

From the mid-70s through to the mid-80s, a vertical approach (Kortese, p.5) emerged through the adoption of a series of Directives that set forth a sector-specific system for specific professions, namely (in chronological adoption order) doctors (1975), lawyers (1977), nurses (1977), dentists and veterinarians (1978), midwives (1980), and architects and pharmacists (1985).[75] Seven professions (all of the above but unfortunately excluding

---

[73] The National Archives, The European Communities (Recognition of Professional Qualifications) (Second General System) Regulations 1996
[74] Koikkalainen, S., Free Movement in Europe: Past and Present, Migration Policy Institute, 21 April 2011
[75] ACE/EAIE professional section of Admissions Officers & Credential evaluators

awyers) are regulated in all Member States and qualifications are subject to the principle
of automatic recognition, a no-questions-asked, carte-blanche access to any prime
destination in the continent they desire, provided that the home country credentials
presented for recognition completely correspond, or are equivalent to, those of the host
country.

For some reason, the profession of attorney-at-law languished through two decades of
litigation and sequential legislation that spoon-fed one right or privilege after another.
Directive 77/249[76] facilitated the exercise of the freedom to provide legal services, but
specifically denied the recognition of professional credentials and freedom of
establishment, which did not come about until 1998 with Directive 98/5 after the seminal
case of *Reinhard Gebhard v Consiglio dell'Ordine degli Avvocati e Procuratori di Milano*
(1995). This is despite clear rulings addressing this issue in *Barreau de Paris v Onno Klopp*
more than a decade earlier, and *Claude Gullung v Conseil de l'ordre des avocats du barreau
de Colmar et de Saverne* in the late 80s.

An intentional quagmire for aspiring migrant lawyers is apparent in *Jean Reyners v Belgian
State* (1974),[77] where the Court of Justice (hereinafter, "the Court") held that the provisions
articulating the freedom of establishment enshrined in the Treaty had only *partial* direct
effect on national law whereby depending on the laws of individual Member States. The
Reyners case was referred to the Court by the Belgian Conseil d'Etat for a preliminary ruling.

[76] Directive 77/249/EEC
[77] Reyners v The Belgium State

The competent authority had obstinately denied attorney Jean Reyners admittance to the bar in that country due to his Dutch citizenship in accordance with Section 428 of their Judicature Act of 1967[78] and, interestingly, to their assertion that the profession "connected organically to the public administration of justice," and therefore wielded "official authority" exempt from the exercise of freedom of establishment under Article 51[79] of the Treaty. The Court ruled in Mr. Reyners' favour affirming that he indeed would not, in his capacity as lawyer, assert such power and, therefore, was free to establish himself in Belgium, thus abolishing the restriction on bar admittance based on nationality enshrined in the said Act.

The principle of mutual recognition was further entrenched by the landmark ruling in *Jean Thieffry v Conseil de l'ordre des avocats*[80] (1977) which, citing *Reyners*, held that "the act of demanding the national diploma prescribed by the legislation of the country of establishment constitutes...a restriction incompatible with the freedom of establishment guaranteed by Article 52 of the Treaty." Attorney Thieffry was thus allowed to practise law in France based on his Belgian credentials.

General System Directives and Recognition of Prior Experience

---

[78] "No one may hold the title of avocat nor practise that profession unless he is Belgian," clearly a prejudicial clause meant to restrict the professional recognition and migration of lawyers.

[79] TFEU, Article 51: "The provisions of this Chapter shall not apply, so far as any given Member State is concerned, to activities which in that State are connected, even occasionally, with the exercise of official authority."

[80] Thieffry v Conseil de l'ordre des avocats

n 21 December 1988, the European Council adopted Directive 89/48[81] establishing a
eneral system" applicable to those professions which are not the subject of specific
irectives, i.e. Sectoral Directives, for the recognition of higher-education diplomas,
ertificates or other evidence of formal qualification "for the taking up or pursuit of a
egulated profession" by self-employed as well as employed persons. It allowed the
ompetent authorities of a Member State to require "adaptation periods" and "aptitude
ests" or the provision of "evidence of professional experience" where the amount of
ducation is deemed insufficient for the practice of a certain profession, as well as evidence
f good conduct.

his was reflected in *Irène Vlassopoulou v Ministerium für Justiz*[82] (1991) where the Court
eld that Member States are obligated to "examine to what extent the knowledge and
ualifications attested by the diploma obtained by the person concerned in his country of
rigin correspond to those required by the rules of the host State; if those diplomas
orrespond only partially, the national authorities in question are entitled to require the
erson concerned to prove that he has acquired the knowledge and qualifications which
re lacking." In spite of 88/48, German authorities had unfairly blocked Ms. Vlassopoulou,
ut the Court came to the rescue providing her a path to recognition. Similarly, *Colegio
Oficial de Agentes de la Propriedad Inmobiliaria v José Luis Aguirre Borrell* (1992) allowed
Member States to require an examination to assess the partial correspondence or

---

Directive 89/48/EEC
Irène Vlassopoulou v Ministerium für Justiz

equivalence of knowledge and skills certified by the diploma or professional qualification to those required by the host country.[83]

These cases established judicial precedent whereby the acquisition of knowledge had to be somehow proven through attestations of previous training and experience over certain periods of time, thus ushering in a new horizontal approach to the recognition of professional qualifications (Kortese, p.5).

Directive 92/51/EEC[84], the second General System Directive, supplemented 89/48 to recognise education as evidenced by diplomas and the like as well as professional experience and training either automatically or, if deemed insufficient, "after compensation" through an adaptation period or aptitude test, per the desire of the migrant who must be allowed to choose between the two by the host country. This Directive also interestingly extends to the employees of those self-employed persons heretofore subject to the foregoing Transitional Directives.

Teresa Fernández v Museo Nacional del Prado[85] (1999) cited and affirmed the provisions of Directives 89/48 and 92/51 in support of the plaintiff migrant's case to require the competent host country authority to assess the practical experience thereof and recognise the terms and conditions of collective labour conventions as "rules regulating a professional activity" in much the same way as a professional organization governs a certain occupation as provided for in 89/48.

---

[83] Colegio Oficial de Agentes de la Propriedad Inmobiliaria v José Luis Aguirre Borrell
[84] Directive 92/51/EEC
[85] Teresa Fernández v Museo Nacional del Prado

he third and last General System Directive (99/42)[86] broadened the scope of the first two

) include experience measured in years during which work was undertaken in a specified

apacity, namely self-employed, business proprietor, manager (described as "deputy of the

roprietor") and employed.

egislators thus took on a vastly liberalised approach to credential recognition going full

ircle from the narrow sole-proprietor tradesmen, up through high-end professional

ervices and specialised medical and dental clinics, apothecaries, architectural offices and

iw firms, and back down again to the heirs of the initial salt-of-the-earth practitioners of

killed vocations.

he SLIM Directive, the PQD and its Modernised Version

า 2001, the foregoing Sectoral Directives and General System Directives were amended

nd simplified in the so-called SLIM Directive (2001/19) requiring Member States to

xamine regulated education, training, and professional experience in the recognition of

rofessional and occupational credentials and, for the first time, incorporating precedential

ulings on third-country qualifications. [87] This is a far cry from the 1960s practice of

ecruiting significant numbers of guest workers through bilateral agreements concluded

vith third countries to work in so-called "3D" conditions, i.e. dirty, dangerous, and dull jobs.

Germany hosted Turks, France brought in Algerians, and former colonial Commonwealth

iation citizens were welcomed in Britain (Koikkalainen).

---

[86] Directive 99/42/EC
[87] Directive 2001/19/EC

Had recognition of all working individuals' past experience as well as third-country qualifications been mandated in the early days of the EEC, perhaps a stronger economic base would have been cultivated buttressing Europe against the detrimental effects of the oil crisis and saving it from the doldrums of the 70s.

On 7 September 2005, the European Parliament and the Council adopted the so-called Professional Qualification Directive[88] ("PQD"; 2005/36) covering both self-employed and employed Member State and third-country nationals and requiring host countries to recognise qualifications, experience and training acquired abroad and provide adaptation periods of supervised training and eligibility to sit for aptitude tests.

Referring specifically to architects and engineers, PQD classifies professional recognition into de facto (unregulated), for which there are no procedures concerning the recognition of qualifications set by EU law, and de jure (regulated), which refers to the right that professionals have to work abroad in a legally regulated profession whereto access is subject to specific professional qualifications differing substantially per Member State.

PQD incorporates the Transitional Directives specifically covering transport and insurance intermediaries adding on statutory auditors and lawyers, both in terms of the freedom to provide services and of establishment. It prescribes minimum training requirements for each of the designated professions for automatic recognition and broadly outlines

---

[88] Directive 2005/36/EC

esignated courses for specific occupations and professional bodies charged with cognising professions.

2D codifies the principle of partial access to professionals if they are fully qualified in their ome Member State but "the differences between the home and host Member State ualifications are so large that the professional would have to go through an entirely new ourse of study to be able to exercise the profession in the host Member State."

his is quite a departure from the restrictive, conservative earlier days of the EEC. It seems s though migrants had a remarkably positive effect on the local societies and economies f the countries where they settled during the five decade-long era spanning from the itification of the Treaty of Rome up to the adoption of this broad-based, liberal, open-door irective. So much so that legislators ventured far and wide from the initial focus on lone raftsmen and entrepreneurs with valuable trades, through four decades of law-making and tigation, the Treaty of Maastricht and its Schengen visa, to finally enfranchise clearly ompetent, qualified, hard-working professionals from all walks of life.

decade later, PQD was modernised into Directive 2013/36[89], which conceptualized the irtual European Professional Card (EPD), an "electronic certificate to allow the cardholder o obtain the recognition of his or her qualifications in a simplified and accelerated nanner"[90] (notice the addition of "or her" in the wording not seen in earlier Directives) hrough exchanges between competent national authorities using the newly created

---

[89] Directive 2013/36/EU
[90] Redondo, A., The modernised Professional Qualifications Directive – The end of crisis-induced nemployment in the EU?, KSLR

Internal Market Information System (IMI), which results in significant reductions in administrative costs and processing time.

For doctors, the modernized PQD guarantees automatic recognition by providing evidence of a minimum of 5,500 hours of training over at least 5 years for basic medical education. It also calls on Member States to limit regulated professions by compiling lists of specific exclusive activities, to justify the need for their regulation and to mutually evaluate them. New professions to be included in the scope of the principle of automatic recognition shall be subject to common training and testing in all Member States. Language skills were also a new target of the modernized PQD. Verification shall only take place after professional credential recognition and be proportional to the activity. Lastly, young professionals shall be given the opportunity under this Directive to undergo traineeships in other Member States in their quest to access regulated professions.

PQD also strengthens patient and consumer safeguards through "an alert mechanism for education and health professions [whereby] the competent authority of the home Member States must inform the competent authorities of all other Member States via IMI of any identified professional…who has been suspended or prohibited from practising…or who has made use of falsified documents" (Rotondo). Protecting the interests of the recipients of the services of migrant professionals is a quantum leap from the constricted scope of the original Directives.

Conclusion

e gradual development of the principle of mutual recognition of professional alifications is rooted in the exponential economic boom of post-war Europe up through e early 1970s. The Directives on recognition during those years provided an opportunity r legislators to yoke the strengths of qualified entrepreneurs in key industries looking to igrate to more promising areas. Unfortunately, the European economy was susceptible to e recessionary effects of the oil crisis, leading legislators to refocus recognition Directives n regulated professions, with the exclusion of attorneys. Gradually, professionals looking establish in another Member State acquired their rights through the judicial process and, adually, individual Member States evolved by incorporating the provisions of relevant irectives into national laws, regulations, and administrative processes. From the *eisegewerbekarte* ("Itinerant Trader's Card") issued to specific migrants in Germany back the 70s, to the modern pan-EU virtual *European Professional Card*, the road to mutual rofessional credential recognition is can be illustrated as triangular in shape starting from narrow apex and stretching outwards to cover a vast expanse of hopeful professionals spiring to new heights in their chosen careers.

QUESTION 5

Explain the nature and scope of the fiduciary duties that equity imposes upon trustees, and
critically analyse the extent to which these duties are founded on the principle explained by
Lord Herschell in Bray v Ford (1896).

Introduction

The nature and scope of fiduciary duties imposed upon trustees by equity are best
described, in the opinion of the author, by the Law Commission's Fiduciary Duties and
Regulatory Rules[91] published in December 1995 which define a fiduciary relationship, as
follows:

"One in which a person undertakes to act on behalf of or for the benefit of another, often
as an intermediary with a discretion of power which affects the interests of the other who
depends on that person for information and advice."

The next section provides four rules governing that relationship, as follows:

- The No Conflict Rule

  A fiduciary is prohibited from placing himself in a position where his own interest
  conflicts with that of his client.

- The No Profit Rule

  A fiduciary is prohibited from profiting from his position at the expense of his client.

- The Undivided Loyalty Rule

---

[91] Bibliography Item No. 1

A fiduciary is prohibited from placing himself in a position where his duty with respect to one client conflicts with that owed to another.

- The Duty of Confidentiality

A fiduciary is prohibited from using information obtained in confidence from his client for his own advantage or that of another.

The extent to which the foregoing principle and accompanying prohibitions are founded on *George Bray v. John Rawlinson Ford (1896)* is apparent in Lord Herschell's statement, as follows:

"An individual in a fiduciary position is neither entitled to profit from, nor allowed to place himself in, a situation where his interest and duty conflict, unless otherwise expressly provided for in the terms of his fiduciary duties, lest he be swayed by interest rather than by duty and alienate those he was bound to protect."[92]

Clearly, the No Conflict and No Profit Rules are articulated here, whilst the Undivided Loyalty Rule is encapsulated in the No Conflict Rule and the Duty of Confidentiality is merely an extension of the No Profit Rule, albeit restricted to the handling of information. In reading these precepts, one visualises a vulnerable individual depending on another to act honestly and in good faith, entrusting in him the wellbeing of his family and estate, and looking to him to safeguard his interests with integrity and loyalty. This, however, is not the situation Messrs. Bray and Ford found themselves in in the late 19th century.

Bibliography Item No. 2

Far from adjudicating on any actual breach of fiduciary duty, *Bray v Ford* is a defamation case of all things that was brought before the House of Lords in 1896 after twice having been tried involving a solicitor, Mr. Ford, accused by one of the governors of an educational institution, Mr. Bray, of violating his fiduciary duty with respect to the same due to his concurrent position as vice-chairman of its council of governors whilst providing paid legal services thereto. That college's articles of association, however, expressly provided for remuneration for services rendered, including those of solicitors, irrespective of whether the service provider held any position within the governance structure thereof, e.g. the vice chairmanship of its council. It is these articles that Lord Herschell was perhaps referring to when he stated "*unless otherwise expressly provided for in the terms of his fiduciary duties*' in his articulation of the principle of fiduciary duty.

Moreover, none of cardinal rules proffered in the Law Commission's publication were ever broken by Mr. Ford throughout the period of his relationship with the college and, as demonstrated in the foregoing, *Bray v Ford* did not deal with any actual breach of fiduciary duty on the part thereof in his capacity as council vice-chairman. Much to the contrary. Lord Herschell pointed out that his role as solicitor to the college predated his appointment to that position by many years, his commitment and loyalty thereto was clearly demonstrated by his decade and a half of service, a portion of which was provided pro bono before 1878, and his fees for legal services had been transparently charged against and properly and usually invoiced to the college under his partnership's auspices after 1878 and up to the year of the suit (1896), and duly recognised as appropriate under its articles of corporation. Therefore, Mr. Bray's quite public accusation of "illegally and improperly" ofiting from his position was baseless and likely brought upon by jealousy.

evertheless, Mr. Bray's libellous conduct did provide posterity, albeit by accident, with e of the foundations upon which was edified the principle of equitable fiduciary duty. is accidental articulation stems from the fact that the nature and scope of fiduciary duty efined by Lord Herschell were provided ancillary to his judgement ordering a retrial for the ppellant as a means to rectify the misdirection of the jury by the appellate judge and not part of any adjudication on any particular violation.

he jury in the court of first instance and, later, the appellate court were both correct in eir judgement against Mr. Bray who, instead of slandering Mr. Ford and dragging his putation through the mud, should have endeavoured to revise the articles of association consultation with his colleagues on the council and table a motion to prohibit Mr. Ford om providing legal services to the institution going forward in so long as he served as vice-hairman thereof.

herefore, *Bray v Ford* was simply a vessel through which a member of the House of Lords as able to quite adeptly articulate the nature and scope of fiduciary duty for legal scholars nd practitioners to quote and expound upon, and unfortunately not a cautionary tale of he perils of fiduciary relationships.

he Wayward Nephew

There is one such historical case, *Wm. Molle, W.S., Trustee of the Rev. John Edgar, Minister of the Gospel at Lymington v Wm. Riddell of Camiestoun, Esq., W.S. (1816)*[93] which predates *Bray v Ford* and, in the opinion of the author, is a cautionary tale truly embodying the nature and scope of fiduciary duty and the perils of unconditional and unverified trust that actually involved a breach thereof duly adjudicated by the trial judge and which should have included the articulation of some guiding principle or benchmark for fiduciaries as provided by Lord Herschell fourscore later.

Edgar v Riddell sheds light on brazen violations of fiduciary duty spanning several decades against a landowning family, which notably included a doctor and a colonel in the armed forces, by a close and trusted member thereof, a blood relative no less, in the reign of King George III.

The year was 1766 anno domini and a certain Scottish landowner Mr. Richard Edgar, Esq. bequeathed his estate to his daughter, Margaret Edgar, the wife of Dr. Hunter, upon his death "in liferent, and to the heirs-male to be procreated of her body, by the present or any subsequent marriage; whom failing, to the heirs-female of her body in fee; whom failing, to my own nearest heirs whatsoever, also in fee, heritably and irredeemably, etc." The crime committed here involved the illegal conveyance of Dr. Hunter's estate by the respondent in this case, Mr. William Riddell, to himself thus provoking the ire of Reverend John Edgar, the appellant in this case and grandnephew and heir of line of Richard Edgar.

---

[93] Bibliography Item No. 3

1779, the Hunters endeavoured to create freeholds for their two estates about the Scottish countryside including that which was inherited from Mr. Edgar by his daughter Margaret wherefor the respondent, the Doctor's nephew and "ordinary man of business," was employed to draft the deeds, which included their four children, Richard Edgar Hunter (the future army colonel), William Hunter, and two daughters, to whom Mr. Riddell was also assigned as tutor-at-law.

Mr. Hunter granted a feu right of the property of that estate to the respondent as trustee who created a liferent disposition of the superiority of the estate providing a vote in favour of another relation, Mr. Robert Riddell, and "then conveyed the remainder of it, which afforded a separate vote, to and in favour of himself in liferent, and Edgar Hunter, his eldest son, and his heirs and assignees, whom failing, to William Hunter, his second son, and his heirs and assignees, heritably in fee." Putting aside the newly-created liferent dispositions, the respondent then on the same day as the foregoing executed the deeds in a manner that reconveyanced the feu of the property, having been made to him in trust, back to the Doctor, under the precise terms in liferent for him and his two sons successively, and their heirs and assignees in fee but granting the eldest son a right to the superiority and the dominium utile of the estate.

Edgar Hunter was in the army where he ascended the ranks to Colonel and entrusted the respondent for the general management of his affairs which, after his death, he utilised to his own advantage as there were no other living descendants, by proclaiming himself Dr. Hunter's heir-at-law, completing a title and entering into possession of both estates.

The appellant Rev. John Edgar, through his trustee Mr. William Molle, filed a lawsuit at court submitting a provision of heir-of-line to Richard Edgar as his grandnephew and to Mrs. Hunter, his daughter, and to Colonel Hunter, her son and heir, "thereupon obtaining a decree of adjudication therefrom in implement against the respondent, whereafter he raised the present action of declarator and reduction, concluding alternately, that it should be found and declared [that] the destination in the reconveyance of the feu right was inserted by the respondent without her authority after the death of Dr. Hunter and because the service of Colonel Hunter, as heir to his mother, was unwarrantably expede by the respondent."

At trial, the respondent attempted to plead his case for drafting and executing instruments, whose effect was to carry the estate to him, by entering parole evidence to establish that his actions were indeed based on verbal instructions from Mrs. Hunter assisted by her husband. This boldfaced lie was rejected by Lord Meadowbank in his judgement, stating: "He need[ed] not dwell on the incompetency to change the legal import of a deed formally executed by parole evidence, or the danger of admitting it, [and] it would shake the title deeds of landed property to give any countenance to the plea, that conveyancers, having a contingent interest in settlements, were bound, on pain of nullity, to produce separate authorities for the terms of the deeds of their clients."

Lord Meadowbank should have continued here in the style of Lord Herschell and articulated, for the sake of posterity, what exactly the fiduciary duties of a conveyancer would be. However, he merely reinforced the illegitimacy of parole evidence as a basis for e formal execution of title deeds to landed property, the inadmissibility thereof in court support of such execution having been found as unwarranted and illegal, and the duty to oduce separate authorities for the terms stipulated in them.

onclusion

ie Riddell case was the perfect opportunity for the House of Lords to lay down a set of iles by which the conduct of conveyancers would be governed. As a trusted member of ie Hunter family charged with managing the legal instruments that legitimised the line of iccession in the estate dating back decades to 1766, as well as with the education of their iildren, Mr. Riddell had edified a relationship in which he undertook to act on behalf of or ir the benefit of the Hunters with a discretion of power which affected their interests, as stablished by the Law Commission, and who depended on him to act honestly and in good iith, entrusting in him the wellbeing of their family and estate, and looking to him to afeguard their interests with integrity and loyalty. Instead, he shrewdly manipulated the ording of the documentation he was hired to draft to extricate lawful heirs and successors ind stealthily enter into possession of the estate to the demise of the family he ipresented, abusing the trust that Colonel Hunter had placed in him for the management f his affairs. He then embarrassed himself in court by attempting to enter parole evidence is unlikely proof of Mrs. Hunter's verbal instructions and approval of his conniving surpation.

he Riddell case and others like it throughout the century preceding the Ford case are better iositioned to provide fiduciaries with a moral compass when carrying out their duties on behalf of their clients. Where Ford was an unfounded accusation wherefrom the relationship between the counterparties was explored by the presiding judge which resulted in the accidental articulation of the principle of fiduciary duty, Riddell was an actual breach of that duty which was duly rebuked and adjudicated by a judge who should have seized on the opportunity to engrave upon the tablets of English common law a set of commandments that would have governed fiduciaries yet unborn.

QUESTION 6

Academy Plus owns and occupies a large building in Bigheantun High Street.

Claude, an expert on local history, is contracted with Academy Plus to deliver a lecture on 'Local Legends'. As Claude begins to speak, a large spotlight falls from the roof of the Academy Plus lecture theatre injuring Claude. The light has recently been installed by Darren, an unqualified electrician who is a nephew of the Principal of Academy Plus.

Ethan, an electrical contractor is then contracted by Academy Plus to install a new spotlight. Ethan connects the new spotlight without switching the electricity supply off. Ethan receives an electric shock and falls off his ladder suffering a broken elbow in the fall.

Farren, the five-year-old daughter of the Academy Plus receptionist, regularly comes to work with her mother. Farren is playing near the window in her mother's office while her mother is busy on the phone and Farren injures her foot on a rusty nail sticking out from a floorboard. Discuss any potential liability in occupiers' liability arising from the above.

The assessment brief question delves into the issue of occupier liability illustrating three cases:

Case I. Liability to a visitor for the act or omission of an independent contractor;

Case II. Liability to an independent contractor for the state of the premises or an act or omission of the occupier; and

Case III. Liability to a child visitor for the same causation as in Case II.

Case I falls under section 2, (4), (b) of the Occupiers' Liability Act 1957[94] (hereinafter "OLA"): "Where damage is caused to a visitor by a danger due to the faulty execution of any work of construction, maintenance or repair by an independent contractor employed by the occupier, the occupier is not to be treated without more as answerable for the danger if in all the circumstances he had acted reasonably in entrusting the work to an independent contractor and had taken such steps (if any) as he reasonably ought in order to satisfy himself that the contractor was competent and that the work had been properly done;" Case II is applicable to OLA, section 2, (3), (b): "An occupier may expect that a person, in the exercise of his calling, will appreciate and guard against any special risks ordinarily incident to it, so far as the occupier leaves him free to do so;" and Case III is a clear-cut OLA, section 1 case whereunder the occupier owed a duty "to his visitors in respect of dangers due to the state of the premises or to things done or omitted to be done on them" compounded by OLA, section 2, (3), (a) obligating him to "be prepared for children to be less careful than adults."

In Case I, a historian expressly invited by the occupier, deemed herein as the owner of the building and operator of the enterprise, to enter the premises that the latter controls, i.e. a lawful invitee per OLA, section 1, (2), subsequently sustained an injury whilst being physically present therein due to an incident involving a fallen ceiling-mounted spotlight that had been installed by an individual unqualified to engage in such work. That person

---

[94] *Occupiers' Liability Act 1957*

as in fact an independent contractor per OLA, section 2, (4), (b) whose blood relation to the principal, deemed herein as an officer in the administration of the occupier's enterprise, effectively blinded the occupier to the risk involved in permitting such an incompetent knucklehead to perform a task obviously not within the scope of his calling whereby a heavy blunt object was affixed overhead in such a way as to expose anyone who happened to be physically present thereunder to the danger of injury should its connection to the ceiling fail. As the occupier's counsel, unfortunately relying solely on his trust for his employee, I would argue in his defence that he had "acted reasonably in entrusting the work" to the nephew and "had taken such steps as he reasonably ought in order to satisfy himself that [the nephew of the trusted employee] was competent and that the work had been properly done" per the foregoing provisions. Moreover, the occupier had arguably been rendered mentally deficient, albeit temporarily, by his misplaced trust making him a moral imbecile, a liability vitiating factor, as defined in the Mental Deficiency Act 1913[95] for the minuscule moment during which he made the ill-fated decision to engage that nincompoop nephew thus actualising a defect of reason defensible citing *R v Clarke 1971*[96]: "The picture painted by the evidence was wholly consistent with this being [an occupier] who retained [his] ordinary powers of reason but who was momentarily absent-minded or confused and acted as [he] did by failing to concentrate properly on what [he] was doing and by failing adequately to use [his] mental powers [due to misplaced trust]." It could also be argued in

---

[5] *Mental Deficiency Act 1913*
[6] *R v Clarke 1971*

his defence that the historian was knowledgeable of the risk involved in standing under hanging spotlight and willingly accepted his exposure to danger per OLA, section 2, (5), "the common duty of care does not impose on an occupier any obligation to a visitor in respect of risks willingly accepted as his by the visitor," thus rendering him a co-contributor to his own injury and, therefore, *volenti non fit injura*. Lord Denning's dicta in *Jones v Livox 1952*[97] could then be applied: "Even though the [historian] did not foresee the possibility of being [injured], nevertheless in the ordinary plain common sense of this [situation], the injury suffered by the [historian] was due in part to the fact that he chose to [stand under the spotlight]." The mere fact that the occupier was not aware of the faulty ceiling connection is a sufficient defence per *Haseldine v Daw 1941*.[98]

Conversely, if I were counsel to the historian, I would accuse the occupier of actionable negligence conjuring Lord Blackburn to the proceedings and stating for the record his dicta in *Dalton v Angus 1881*[99]: "A person causing something to be done, the doing of which casts on him a duty, cannot escape from the responsibility attaching on him of seeing that duty performed by delegating it to a contractor [and] cannot thereby relieve himself from liability to those injured by the failure to perform it." I would add "properly" to the end of that dicta per OLA, section 2, (4), (b) thus demonstrating to the court that the historian's injury had effectively been sustained as a result of the occupier's failure to fulfil the common duty of care "to see that the visitor will be reasonably safe in using the premises for the purposes

---

[97] *Jones v Livox 1952*
[98] *Haseldine v Daw 1941*
[99] *Dalton v Angus 1881*

r which he is invited or permitted by the occupier to be there" (OLA, section 2, (2)). An ven more ambitious prosecution could go as far as accusing the occupier, his employee, ne nephew and the spotlight manufacturer as contributory negligent cotortfeasors as efined in section 1 of the Law Reform (Contributory Negligence) Act 1945[100] reinforced by ord Denning's dicta in *Davies v Swan 1949*[101]: "There are two aspects to apportioning esponsibility...in an action for negligence, the respective causative potency of what they ave done, and their respective blameworthiness," whereunder (i) the employee's ecommendation to the occupier of his nephew as contractor to undertake the work, (ii) ne omission of proper care by the occupier to ensure his competence, qualification and roper execution of the work, (iii) the incompetence and negligence of the nephew, and (iv) ny defect in the manufacture of the brackets, bolts, fittings, etc. of the spotlight, would be neasured individually in terms of their respective causative potency in order to fairly pportion blame. In case the existence of an express or implied agreement between any of hese parties with regard to the installation of the spotlight in question should surface at rial, then section 2, (2) of the Unfair Contract Terms Act 1977[102], "a person cannot by eference to any contract term...exclude or restrict his liability for death or personal injury esulting from negligence," would be applicable.

n Case II, an electrician contractor licenced by the foregoing occupier to enter the said oremises for the purpose of replacing the said fallen spotlight (i.e. a lawful licensee per OLA,

---

[100] Law Reform (Contributory Negligence) Act 1945
[101] *Davies v Swan 1949*
[102] Unfair Contract Terms Act 1977

section 1, (2)) subsequently sustained an injury resulting from receiving an electric shock due to his own failure to disconnect the power source prior to engaging in the contracted works. The occupier would likely be held not liable for the injury sustained by the electrical service provider dispatchee according to OLA, section 2, (3), (b), "an occupier may expect that a person, in the exercise of his calling, will appreciate and guard against any special risks ordinarily incident to it, so far as the occupier leaves him free to do so," as any competent electrician would be expected to be cognisant of the danger involved in handling electrical equipment and live wires. Ascertaining the status of the spotlight's connection to the power source would arguably have to precede any other consideration in the step-by-step planning of the procedures necessary to properly and safely replace the spotlight, and electric shock is definitely a risk "ordinarily incident" to his calling. I would enter into evidences local electrician trade school vocational training programme textbooks and manuals as well as the spotlight manufacturer's installation instruction and owner' manuals to demonstrate to the court that tradesman's incompetence in the face of danger. In both cases, per *Gwilliam v Trust 2002*,[103] the occupier may not have taken "reasonable steps to satisfy himself that the contractor carried liability insurance," which would have provided evidence of his "reputability and competence," but that is irrelevant since he was totally blinded by trust in Case I and satisfied by the contractor's self-declaration as a

---

[103] *Gwilliam v Trust 2002*

ualified electrician in Case II, therefore, insurance would not have made a difference in

ther situation.

o summarise, I invoke Lord Brooke's dicta in *Bottomley v Todmorden 2003*[104] in which he

roclaimed that (i) occupier liability for the negligence of an independent contractor is

tiated "provided that he had exercised reasonable care" in his engagement, (ii) occupier

ability is vitiated in case of an injury sustained by an independent contractor resulting from

the way in which the work [was] being carried out, and (iii) where the work is "regarded

y the law as being [extra-hazardous], a duty is imposed on the [occupier] to see that care

taken; and [he] is vicariously liable for any negligence of the independent contractor."

ased on items (i) and (ii) of the foregoing, the occupier is discharged of liability in both

ases involving the fallen ceiling spotlight and its replacement, but liable for item (iii) should

he court find that the installation of a ceiling spotlight constitutes in itself an extra-

azardous activity.

ase III, liability actualised with respect to a child visitor, involves an incident whereby the

hild of an employee of the foregoing occupier visiting the premises sustained an injury

esulting from an exposed nail protruding from a floorboard. The fact that the employee

egularly brought the child to the premises, which the occupier ought to have been

nowledgeable of, effectively estopped him from claiming that he had never led the

mployee to believe that the child was permitted to enter the premises, per *Edwards v*

---

[104] *Bottomley v Todmorden 2003*

Railway Executive 1952,[105] and no action was ever taken by the occupier to stop the employee from bringing the child to the premises, per *Lowery v Walker 1910*.[106]

Contrastingly, as counsel to the occupier, I would argue that his duty of care was discharged as the child in question was accompanied by an adult and a prudent parent would be expected to check for danger and constantly supervise their child per *Phipps v Rochester 1955*[107] and *Simkiss v Rhondda Borough Council 1983*.[108] OLA, section 2, (3) could in his defence be interpreted in such a way as to demonstrate parental negligence that contributed to the child's injury: "The circumstances [surrounding the incident] include the degree of care [by the occupier], and [the degree] of want of care [by the employee], which would ordinarily be looked for in such a visitor [who brings a small child to a workplace as he ought to] be prepared for children to be less careful than adults [and be expected], in the exercise of his [employment], [to] appreciate and guard against any special risks ordinarily incident to [leaving a child unattended at a workplace], so far as the occupier leaves him free to do so," therefore, *volenti non fit injura*. The parent ought to have known, as any reasonable person should know, "that young children [are] of a very inquisitive and frequently mischievous disposition, and are likely to meddle with whatever happens to come within their reach" (*Cooke v Midland 1909*).[109] Judgement for the defendant!

---

[105] *Edwards v Railway Executive 1952*
[106] *Lowery v Walker 1910*
[107] *Phipps v Rochester 1955*
[108] *Simkiss v Rhondda Borough Council 1983*
[109] *Cooke v Midland 1909*

ference was made to the following for general guidance on relevant precedential case

w:

McBride and R. Bagshaw, *Tort Law*, Fourth Edition (Chapter on Occupiers' Liability),

sex, Pearson Education Limited, 2012

QUESTION 7

Critically discuss the following statement:

"The purpose behind the principle of precedent is to ensure legal certainty."

_____

Introduction

The principle, or doctrine, of judicial precedent, or stare decisis, is described in The Encyclopedia of Canadian Laws as the requirement of a judge to follow the ruling of another judge of the same, or higher, court on the same issue in order to ensure a measure of security and stability in a legal system based on common law, the body of which being developed over time through the accumulation of court judgments. In arguing whether this doctrine preserves legal certainty, the starting point should be the words "security and stability" in the foregoing definition.[110] Turner (2005) and Weatherill (2012) describe legal certainty in their textbooks as attained when the so-called rule of law is guaranteed through a predictable, stable, generally applicable, foreseeable, precise and fair set of rules, which in our common law society refers to precedential court rulings, established to provide the governed with the assurance of reasonable expectations, limited retroactivity, and protection (i.e. non-withdrawal) of acquired rights, whether basic, fundamental, human, commercial or preferential, thus allowing those subject to the law of the land to regulate

_____

[110] Encyclopedia of Canadian Laws

eir conduct and go about their business with the certainty that rules will be followed with

otection from the arbitrary exercise of state power.[111]

article published by the Law Society argues that, in the wake of Brexit, we are now faced

th the titanic task of removing EU law from the UK legal framework, the greatest concern

which is whether legal certainty will be preserved with regard to jurisdiction, judicial

ecedent and statutes, as well as access to courts and authorities by UK consumers and

all business operators, or other vulnerable stakeholders, who in disputes or other

rcumstances would no longer be allowed to have their cases heard in their home law,

hich would in essence remove the assurances, security, stability and predictability

ovided by judicial precedent and jurisprudence, the key elements of legal certainty in a

mmon law system.[112]

illiam James, reporting for Reuters, provides a solution in the form a May government

oposal to convert the EU corpus lex into UK law through the tentatively-dubbed "Great

epeal Bill" to be put forth before Parliament in the spring. If enacted, James goes on, it will

ake all EU laws UK laws, repeal the European Communities Act of 1972, and give ministers

he power to change existing laws in an effort to maintain legal certainty for businesses

hrough continuity so that they could continue operating across EU borders knowing the

---

[11] C. Turner, *Unlocking EU Law*, Hodder Arnold, London, 2005, p. 68; S. Weatherill, *Cases & Materials on EU aw*, Oxford University Press, Oxford, 2012, p.132

[12] The Law Society

rules have not changed, and providing fairness and assurances that rights and obligation will not be subject to sudden change.[113]

Creating Legal Certainty for Canada's Aboriginal Peoples

Efforts by the state to ensure legal certainty to vulnerable members of society is not new The following historical case deals with the establishment of a legal framework over th course of several centuries based on treaties, a royal decree, Parliamentary legislation an Supreme Court rulings specifically to ensure legal certainty for the aboriginal peoples c Canada, groups of particularly vulnerable stakeholders.

The interests of local governments and businesses, natural resource developers in th Canadian wilderness and other stakeholders often clash with those of aboriginal people who, Thomas Isaac and Anthony Knox of Canadian law firm Thomas Isaac, McCarth Tétrault LLP summarize in 2004 in an article for the New Brunswick Law Journal, ar organized in bands or tribes governed by councils and chiefs looking to safeguard specifi "treaty rights" relating to the cession of land ("aboriginal title") by the British Crown, an subsequently by the Canadian federal government, to individual bands, as well as right relating to hunting, fishing and trapping in specified territories in return for peace with European settlers as articulated in treaties, some dating as far back as the 17th century.[11]

CRIAW, a feminist Indigenous organization, noted that, while a few treaties were enterec

---

[113] W. James, "Britain targets legal certainty with plan to convert EU law after Brexit," Reuters, 30 March 2017

[114] T. Isaac, A. Knox, McCarthy Tétrault LLP, *Canadian Aboriginal Law: Creating Certainty in Resource Development*, University of New Brunswick Law Journal, Vol. 53, 2004

to to encourage peaceful relations and forge strategic alliances, like the "Peace and iendship Treaties" concluded between 1725 and 1779 in the Atlantic maritime region, thers such as the "Numbered Treaties" in Ontario, the Prairies and the Northwest Territory etween 1871 and 1921 involved the ceding or surrendering of rights to vast territories in xchange for rights that included reserve lands, farming equipment and animals, annual ayments, ammunition, clothing, alcohol and medicine, as well as rights relating to fishing, apping and hunting.[115] This is echoed in the Indigenous and Northern Affairs Canada fficial website. Ultimately, these treaty rights, while not specified, were recognized and eaffirmed in Section 35 of the Constitution Act of 1982, which served as the basis for ubsequent Supreme Court of Canada cases that clearly articulate the rights, obligations nd roles of the aboriginal peoples themselves and those of governments and corporations poking to exploit natural resources in areas where aboriginals live, hunt, fish, trap, etc. with espect to them thus ensuring legal certainty.[116]

he Canadian Encyclopedia describes official recognition of the aboriginal peoples as takeholders in the New World as dating back to the Royal Proclamation of 1763 by King George III, which provided for aboriginal land claims and self-government, recognized boriginal rights and imposed a fiduciary duty of care on the British Crown with respect hereto. As such, it has been labelled an "Indian Magna Carta" that contributed to the American Revolution in late 1770s due to its cession of a massive territory west of

[115] Canadian Research Institute for the Advancement of Women, *Colonialism and its Impacts*
[116] Indigenous and Northern Affairs Canada, *Treaty Rights*

Appalachian Mountains as reserves for indigenous tribes angering the colonists, mostly of British decent at the time, who desired western expansion. With regards to aboriginal rights, the Proclamation states explicitly that "aboriginal people reserved all lands not ceded by or purchased from them":

"And whereas it is just and reasonable, and essential to our Interest, and the Security of our Colonies, that the several Nations or Tribes of Indians with whom We are connected, and who live under our Protection, should not be molested or disturbed in the Possession of such Parts of Our Dominions and Territories as, not having been ceded to or purchased by Us, are reserved to them, or any of them, as their Hunting Grounds."[117]

Legislative Framework

The Library of Parliament's official website states that, over a century later, the British North America Act of 1867, the so-called Canada Constitution Act enacted by the British Parliament to establish a governmental framework for the administration of dominions in North America, transferred responsibility for Canada's aboriginal peoples from the British Crown to the Canadian federal government, declaring all aboriginal peoples and their lands under the jurisdiction of Parliament.[118] The infamous Indian Act of 1876 was an attempt to codify the rights provided to aboriginal peoples by the foregoing Proclamation. Its infamy

---

[117] The Canadian Encyclopedia, *Royal Proclamation of 1763*
[118] Library of Parliament, *Federal-Provincial Jurisdiction and Aboriginal Peoples*

ems from discriminatory clauses pertaining to enfranchisement, registers, the English

nguage, education for entering "civilized" society, taxes, etc.[119]

ese Acts unfortunately failed to fully provide legal certainty to aboriginal peoples, but this

rpus lex set forth by our predecessors and lessons learned throughout the ensuing

entury would culminate into the articulation of Section 35 of the Constitution Act of 1982,

law enacted following the patriation of the British North America Act of 1867 from the

itish Parliament to the Canadian Parliament by Prime Minister Trudeau and Queen

izabeth II in 1981:

GHTS OF THE ABORIGINAL PEOPLES OF CANADA

ecognition of existing aboriginal and treaty rights

5. (1) The existing aboriginal and treaty rights of the aboriginal peoples of Canada are

ereby recognized and affirmed.

efinition of "aboriginal peoples of Canada"

2) In this Act, "aboriginal peoples of Canada" includes the Indian, Inuit and Métis peoples

f Canada.

and claims agreements

3) For greater certainty, in subsection (1) "treaty rights" includes rights that now exist by

vay of land claims agreements or may be so acquired.

boriginal and treaty rights are guaranteed equally to both sexes

---

[119] Indigenous and Northern Affairs Canada, *Resolving Aboriginal Claims - A Practical Guide to Canadian Experiences*

(4) Notwithstanding any other provision of this Act, the aboriginal and treaty rights referred

to in subsection (1) are guaranteed equally to male and female persons.

Legal Certainty Through Judicial Precedent Based on Statute

Section 35 effectively constitutes the pushing of the legislative reset button that would

trigger a series of consecutive Supreme Court of Canada cases that dealt precisely with the

protection of aboriginal rights based thereon. Maria Morellato of Canadian law firm Blake,

Cassels & Graydon LLP, writing for the National Centre for First Nations Governance,

describes the process by which aboriginal peoples acquired legal certainty through judicial

precedent as being triggered by Ronald Edward Sparrow v. Her Majesty The Queen (R. v.

Sparrow, 1990; "R" refers to "Regina" or "Rex," i.e. "the Crown"), the first Supreme Court

of Canada case that specifically cited s. 35 to finally enshrine the fiduciary duty of the federal

government with respect to aboriginal peoples and articulate their rights:[120]

"The appellant was charged in 1984 under the Fisheries Act with fishing with a drift net

longer than that permitted by the terms of his Band's Indian food fishing licence. He

admitted that the facts alleged constitute the offence, but defended the charge on the basis

that he was exercising an existing aboriginal right to fish and that the net length restriction

contained in the Band's licence was invalid in that it was inconsistent with s. 35(1) of the

Constitution Act, 1982. The appellant was convicted. The trial judge found that an aboriginal

---

[120] M. Morellato, Blake, Cassels & Graydon LLP, *THE CROWN'S CONSTITUTIONAL DUTY TO CONSULT AND ACCOMMODATE ABORIGINAL AND TREATY RIGHTS*, 2008

ght could not be claimed unless it was supported by a special treaty and that s. 35 is applicable."

he ruling was appealed, dismissed, overturned, appealed again and cross-appealed until nally the Supreme Court of Canada held that:

ection 35(1) of the Constitution Act, 1982 , at the least, provides a solid constitutional ase upon which subsequent negotiations can take place and affords aboriginal peoples onstitutional protection against provincial legislative power. [It] is to be construed in a urposive way. A generous, liberal interpretation is demanded given that the provision is to ffirm aboriginal rights.

Legislation that affects the exercise of aboriginal rights will be valid if it meets the test for ustifying an interference with a right recognized and affirmed under s. 35(1) [which] ncorporates the government's responsibility to act in a fiduciary capacity with respect to boriginal peoples and so import some restraint on the exercise of sovereign power. Federal ower must be reconciled with federal duty and the best way to achieve that reconciliation s to demand the justification of any government regulation that infringes upon or denies boriginal rights.

The first question to be asked is whether the legislation in question has the effect of nterfering with an existing aboriginal right. Courts must be careful to avoid the application of traditional common law concepts of property as they develop their understanding of the sui generis" nature of aboriginal rights.

"If a prima facie interference is found, the analysis moves to the issue of justification. [Is there a valid legislative objective?"[121]

The foregoing academic exercise to be undertaken by any provincial or municipal government when drafting legislation or regulations described in the foregoing became known as the "Sparrow Test."

Sparrow Test

Isaac and Knox (2004) name the case Dorothy Marie Van der Peet v. Her Majesty The Queen (R. v. Van der Peet, 1995) as next in line in the quest for legal certainty. It cites s. 35 and R. v. Sparrow in its argument and articulates for the first time a "justificatory test laid out in R. v. Sparrow" to determine the extent to which aboriginal rights may be regulated or infringed:

"The appellant, a native, was charged with selling 10 salmon caught under the authority of an Indian food fish licence, contrary to s. 27(5) of the British Columbia Fishery (General) Regulations, which prohibited the sale or barter of fish caught under such a licence. The trial judge held that the aboriginal right to fish for food and ceremonial purposes did not include the right to sell such fish and found the appellant guilty."

A subsequent appeal was dismissed, but the Supreme Court of Canada held that that appeal should be dismissed:

---

[121] Judgments of the Supreme Court of Canada, R. v. Sparrow [1990] 1 SCR 1075

purposive analysis of s. 35(1) must take place in light of the general principles applicable to the legal relationship between the Crown and aboriginal peoples. This relationship is a fiduciary one and a generous and liberal interpretation should accordingly be given in favour of aboriginal peoples. Any ambiguity as to the scope and definition of s. 35(1) must be resolved in favour of aboriginal peoples.

Aboriginal rights existed and were recognized under the common law. They were not created by s. 35(1), but subsequent to s. 35(1) they cannot be extinguished. They can, however, be regulated or infringed consistent with the justificatory test laid out in R. v. Sparrow.

Section 35(1) provides the constitutional framework through which the fact that aboriginals lived on the land in distinctive societies[122], with their own practices, customs and traditions, is acknowledged and reconciled with the sovereignty of the Crown."[123]

Prima Facie Infringement

Isaac and Knox (2004) continue with the seminal case of Donald Gladstone and William Gladstone v. Her Majesty The Queen (R. v. Gladstone, 1996), which cited R. v. Sparrow and applied the so-called "Sparrow test" to determine whether a prima facie infringement of aboriginal rights by the state had taken place:

---

[122] The term "distinct society" was proliferated throughout the 1980s and early 90s in Canada in support of the Quebec sovereignty agenda. It was inserted here to establish a judicial precedent linking the plight of the aboriginals to that of the French Quebec nationalists. A referendum for the independence of Quebec was held in the same year as R. v. Van der Peet and failed.
[123] Judgements of the Supreme Court of Canada, R. v. Van der Peet [1996] 2 SCR 507

"The accused were charged under s. 61(1) of the Fisheries Act with attempting to se
herring spawn on kelp caught without the proper licence contrary to s. 20(3) of the Pacifi
Herring Fishery Regulations. They had shipped a large quantity to the Vancouver area an
approached a fish dealer with a sample to see if he was 'interested'. One of the accused, o
arrest, produced an Indian food fish licence permitting him to harvest 500 pounds. Th
Supreme Court of British Columbia and the Court of Appeal upheld the convictions.

"The Sparrow test for determining whether the government has infringed aboriginal right
involves (1) asking whether the legislation has the effect of interfering with an existin
aboriginal right and (2) determining whether the limitation (i) was unreasonable, (i
imposed undue hardship, (iii) denied the right holders their preferred means of exercising
that right.

"Justification of infringements of aboriginal rights involves a two‑part test. The government
must demonstrate that: (1) it was acting pursuant to a valid legislative objective; and (2) its
actions were consistent with its fiduciary duty towards aboriginal peoples.

"The appellants demonstrated a prima facie interference with their aboriginal
rights...Under the regulatory scheme, they can harvest for commercial purposes only to the
limited extent allowed by the government."[124]

Exclusivity to Aboriginal Lands

---

[124] Judgements of the Supreme Court of Canada, R. v. Gladstone [1996] 2 SCR 723

stly, Isaac and Knox (2004) present another landmark case where a massive territory in itish Columbia was claimed by an aboriginal band. In Delgamuukw v. Her Majesty The ueen in Right of the Province of British Columbia and The Attorney General of Canada 997), the Royal Proclamation of 1763, Sparrow, Van der Peet and Gladstone were cited articulate exclusivity with regard to aboriginal lands as flowing from the definition of original title as the right to exclusive use and occupation. This ruling enshrined the federal vernment's "duty to consult" aboriginal peoples regarding the use of their lands for atural resource development and other applications, and its "duty to accommodate original title," thus reaffirming the requirement of the Crown to justify any infringement their rights and reinforcing legal certainty.

he appellants, all Gitksan and Wet'suwet'en hereditary chiefs, claimed separate portions 58,000 square kilometres in British Columbia. British Columbia counterclaimed for a eclaration that the appellants have no right or interest in and to the territory or ternatively, that the appellants' cause of action ought to be for compensation from the overnment of Canada.

At trial, the appellants' claim was based on their historical use and "ownership" of one or ore of the territories. In addition, the Gitksan Houses have an "adaawk" which is a ollection of sacred oral tradition about their ancestors, histories and territories. The Vet'suwet'en each have a "kungax" which is a spiritual song or dance or performance which es them to their land. Both of these were entered as evidence on behalf of the appellants. he most significant evidence of spiritual connection between the Houses and their territory was a feast hall where the Gitksan and Wet'suwet'en people tell and retell their stories and identify their territories to remind themselves of the sacred connection that they have with their lands. The feast has a ceremonial purpose but is also used for making important decisions.

"The trial judge did not accept the appellants' evidence of oral history of attachment to the land. He dismissed the action against Canada, dismissed the plaintiffs' claims for ownership and jurisdiction and for aboriginal rights in the territory."[125]

In the appeal to the Supreme Court of Canada, the Court ruled that:

"Aboriginal title is *sui generis*, and so distinguished from other proprietary interests, and characterized by several dimensions. It is inalienable and cannot be transferred, sold or surrendered to anyone other than the Crown. Another dimension of aboriginal title is its sources: its recognition by the Royal Proclamation, 1763 and the relationship between the common law which recognizes occupation as proof of possession and systems of aboriginal law pre-existing assertion of British sovereignty. Finally, aboriginal title is held communally."[126]

Conclusion

The last line above essentially connects King George III's Proclamation together with s. 35 and the Supreme Court rulings to set legal certainty in stone for these peoples effectively

---

[125] The legal representatives of B.C. Cattlemen's Association et al., Skeena Cellulose Inc., and Alcan Aluminum Ltd., a multinational conglomerate, were intervenors.
[126] Judgements of the Supreme Court of Canada, R. v. Delgamuukw [1997] 3 SCR 1010

vering over 230 years of jurisprudence. Based on the foregoing, it is evident that the original peoples of Canada are guaranteed ample legal certainty by the Crown through e rule of law, particularly through its duty to consult and duty of fiduciary care, based on edictable, stable, generally applicable, foreseeable, precise and fair legislative and nstitutional statutes and precedential court rulings engendering assurances of asonable expectations, limited retroactivity, and protection (i.e. non-withdrawal) of eaty rights relating to the exclusive use of land, fishing, hunting, trapping and commerce, us allowing them to regulate their conduct and go about their business with the certainty at laws will be followed with protection from the arbitrary exercise of state power.

QUESTION 8

Critically analyse the methods by which legal & equitable mortgages might be created sinc

1925. What was the purpose of the 1925 reforms?

Introduction

For centuries, mortgages could take any form but, most commonly, loans on property wer

collateralized by the transfer of legal ownership thereof from the obligor to the obligee, th

former in this transaction in effect losing proprietary interest in res but retaining a singula

equitable right in personam of return of ownership, i.e. the transfer back of the property

upon loan reimbursement.[1] Failure to do so, however, would immediately extinguish tha

right thus placing the obligor in a grossly subordinated position versus the obligee a

common law. The Court of Chancery in the 19th century struck a balance in the obligor'

favour imposing upon all mortgages the equitable right of redemption which curtailed o

even overrode the mortgagee's heretofore inherent right to possession by transfer of title

upon mortgage deed execution, even if its provisions deliberately placed the mortgagor a

a disadvantage such as restricting redemption to the end of the loan term.[2] This is merel

one example of the series of successive steps taken to reform property law in the judiciar

and legislature starting from the mid-nineteenth century and culminating to the Law o

Property Act 1925 enacted in an attempt to create a more level playing field between the

mortgagor and the mortgagee by articulating limited means by which security interests i

property could be established, namely legal mortgages, equitable mortgages, i.e. charges

way of legal mortgage, and other equitable charges.[3] The following is a synopsis and
critique of each type.

gal mortgages

e Law of Property Act, sections 85 to 87 provide the foundation for establishing security
terests in land either by (i) a demise[4] over a legal estate or interest, (ii) a subdemise over
lease on a legal estate, or (iii) a charge by way of legal mortgage, each of which requires a
eed and official registration for taking effect at law.[5] Regarding mortgaging freeholds,
hich are estates in fee simple absolute, the highest form of property ownership in any
ommon law jurisdiction, a new mortgage must be either a demise for a term of years
bsolute subject to cesser[6] upon redemption, or a charge by deed, whereby the mortgagee
as the right to the physical possession of the title deed and other attestations of ownership
s security. If a mortgage is the vehicle for the conveyance of an estate, it must (i) take the
orm of a demise, (ii) without impeachment for waste,[7] (iii) over a term of three thousand
ears, (iv) with a deed of defeasance[8] and other assurance that vests the estate in the
ortgagee subject to redemption. Section 86 regards mortgaging leaseholds, which is
dentical to the foregoing except that the mortgage must be a duly licensed subdemise
whose term of years absolute is at least one day shorter than the lease term vested in the
ortgagor, at least ten days less in case a mortgage is the vehicle for leasehold assignment.
ection 87 essentially makes mortgages by demise exactly the same as charges by way of
egal mortgage. I assume that the wording "shall have the same protection, powers and
emedies" with regard to the mortgagee in item (1) thereof also implies "subject to cesser

upon redemption," or the equitable right of redemption. The problem that arises from these statutes is the relationship created by the demise, which is essentially a leasehold right on the charged property, between mortgagor and mortgagee as one of tenant and landlord, respectively, providing to the latter "inherent rights to possession and to grant subsidiary interests"[9] such as subletting. The demise expressly "vests" the estate in the mortgagee thus involving a veritable transfer of the mortgaged property, whereas the charge by way of legal mortgage merely creates the mortgage "in favour" of the same and bestows a "right to take proceedings," or legal recourse, as security. The weaker cousin of these two types of mortgages is the puisne mortgage, a legal subsequent mortgage[10] on unregistered land which is unsecured due to possession of title deed by the mortgagee of the original or prior mortgage and subject to overreaching and barring of right of redemption in the event of default on the prior mortgage.[11] Alas, the mortgage by demise, which for centuries conveyed the charged property to the obligee upon execution of a mortgage in the form of, quite interestingly, a three thousand year leasehold subjecting the same to foreclosure, repossession or sale by the obligee in the event of default, and then conveyed it back to the obligor upon redemption, has been, thankfully, largely eradicated from society and rendered obsolete by a series of legislation throughout the 20th century. We are therefore left with charges by way of legal mortgage and other equitable charges, as outlined below.

Equitable charges

hilst a mortgage by demise grants the obligee the immediate right of ownership in case

default, an equitable charge is a security interest that only provides the right to seize

curitised real property or personalty realisable by way of the judicial process,[12] however,

e terms "mortgage" and "charge" are at times used interchangeably by judges in their

lings.[13] Equitable charges are formed either by way of mortgage or not. Those with

ortgages involve the binding intention to create a security in favour of the mortgagee by

videncing a contract to that end without actually conferring the legal estate or title

ereon, whereas the mortgage-free charges expressly or constructively appropriate

roperty towards the discharge of an obligation conferring on the obligee the right of

ealisation by judicial process through receivership or sale order as evidenced in the loan

greement.[14] It is this contractual right to judicial process in the event of default on the

nderlying debt or obligation, or failure to satisfy the same in violation of contractual terms

nd conditions, that render charges equitable in form and effect. This contrasts with

ortgages, which actually vest proprietary rights in the obligee as evidenced in the deed.

he only two remedies at equity provided to a chargee are (i) sale, whereby the charged

roperty is seized by court order in the event of default and sold to cover the obligation

vith any residual value held in constructive trust for the chargor, and (ii) appointment of a

eceiver also by court order. Contrastingly, mortgagees are entitled at common law to

oreclosure and possession in the event of some breach of the obligation.[15] In its purest

orm, the equitable mortgage is a sui generis security interest known as a "mortgage by

assignment" under which the chargee is provided a direct interest in the charged property as security for the debt or obligation with remedies at equity.[16] A mortgage can be forma

where the parties duly draft an official deed and register it, or informal, where the obligo

simply deposits the title deed and other evidentiary ownership documentation with th

obligee as security but without officially transferring it; a mortgage can be create

accidentally, where the mortgagor "purports to create a legal mortgage [of] any equitable

interest" he has in the property, or deliberately, where the parties assign the mortgagee

interest "in the same way, and under the same principles, as chattels or choses in action

with a clause for reassignment thereof upon redemption."[17] Please note that the label

"charge" and "mortgage" were deliberately interchanged herein to emphasize the

sameness of the instruments in form and practice, under which "the proprietary right i

contingent on the underlying debt not being paid and an application being made to seize

the charged property,"[18] and where the charges are assumed as fixed, meaning that they

are securitized by appropriating the charged asset or property that is clearly identified anc

designated towards the reimbursement of the obligation thus creating a proprietary

interest defeasible thereupon.[19] There are also floating charges outside the scope of this

brief due to their encumbrance upon non-land interests such as assets, chattels, choses in

action, book debts and stocks.

Equity of Redemption and Possession

One of the key areas of mortgage reform is the equitable right of redemption, which was

routinely "clogged" through some limitation provided for in the mortgage deed. The

landmark case Fairclough v Swan Brewery Co., Ltd. (1912) is a classic example of this. The ortgage deed included a clause that prohibited redemption, and thus forced the payment

interest on the underlying loan, until the last six weeks of the 21-year term. In his ruling,

rd Macnaghten stated that "equity will not permit any device or contrivance being part

the mortgage transaction or contemporaneous with it to prevent or impede

demption."[20] However, in Knightsbridge Estates v Byrne (1939), citing Fairclough,[21] the

ourt declined to unnecessarily interfere with the freedom of contract of the mortgagor,

ho had agreed to a 40-year term at a fixed rate of interest, and established that an overly

ngthy redemption period "is not necessarily a clog" on the equitable right of redemption

d ruling to annul such a mortgage deed provision would create an "impediment to

usiness." Despite this right at equity, there is ample precedent establishing that an obligee

a charge by way of mortgage has an inherent right at common law to claim possession

at is not contingent upon obligor default, unless otherwise provided for. Four-Maids v

udley Marshall (1957), Birmingham Citizens v Caunt (1962) and Mobile Oil v Rawlinson

982) are examples of cases where the Court reaffirmed this right and refused to even

rant the chargor sufficient time to remedy his violation.[22] Section 101 of the Law of

roperty Act 1925 confers the power of sale to a mortgage deed as a remedy to default

ithout judicial recourse, and Section 88 provides that, upon the sale of a repossessed

roperty underlying a defaulted obligation, the chargor's interest therein is overreached

nd transferred to the proceeds. Interestingly, Section 103 gives a chargor in arrears three

whole months to repay the capital but only two to pay the interest starting from the date

f receipt of peremptory notice from the chargee before triggering the power of sale, which is also exercisable in the event of "a breach of some provision contained in the mortgage deed...other than and besides a covenant for payment of the mortgage money or interest thereon."[23] This perhaps opens the door to arbitrary foreclosure and repossession, unless the deed spells out what would constitute a "breach" and the remedies in the event thereof.

Conclusion

The preceding text outlines the principal means by which property is mortgaged or encumbered by loans or interests in the post-1925 era. Society has done away with the vestiges of the bygone eras, the mortgages by leasehold over terms of thousands of years vesting rights of possession in the mortgagee, and supported the development of fair and equitable arrangements. The equitable charge by way of legal mortgage, as described above, is a solid financial instrument that elegantly evolved over time to create a favourable lender-borrower relationship whereby underlying property is appropriated to provide security and assurance of due redemption, which can occur at any time during the mortgage term. The notion of pledging as collateral the very object of a loan is true genius in its simplicity and democratic nature, for if the value of the property is higher than the amount of principal borrowed, then indeed a strong foundation for a loan is created. However, subsequent or multiple mortgages on the same property or the so-called puisne mortgages should be banned, as they ultimately lead to avarice, overspending, overcharging of interest, heavy financial burdens and stress on mortgagors and their families, and little or no security to the lender in the event of prior or original mortgage default.

REFERENCES

Law Commission, Land Mortgages, (Law Com No 99, 1986) para 2.1-2.2.

"Clog on the Right to Redeem," Columbia Law Review, Vol. 12, No. 7 (1912), pp. 627-629.

Law Commission, Land Mortgages, (Law Com No 99, 1986) para 2.3-2.4.

A transfer of the real property by lease or let; obsolete form of mortgage.

Law Commission, Land Mortgages, (Law Com No 99, 1986) paragraph 2.6.

Cessation or termination.

May not be sued for any change in the condition of the property that diminishes or destroys its value.

A document that terminates the effect of an existing document such as a deed, bond or contract.

Law Commission, Land Mortgages, (Law Com No 99, 1986) para 3.4.

10 A second or third mortgage, etc. subordinate to the prior or original mortgage.

11 Land Charges Act 1925, s. 22.

12 Falcon Chambers, Fisher and Lightwood's Law of Mortgage (11th ed., Butterworths, 2002), p. 25.

13 Slade J, Siebe Gorman v Barclays Bank (1979).

14 Buckley LJ, Swiss Bank Corp v Lloyds Bank (1982).

15 A. Hudson, Equity & Trusts, 8th ed. (Oxon, UK: Routledge, 2014), pp. 955-958.

16 Law Commission, Land Mortgages, (Law Com No 99, 1986) para 2.7.

17 Ibid para 2.8.

18 A. Hudson, Equity & Trusts, 8th ed. (Oxon: Routledge, 2014), p. 957.

19 Ibid p. 958

20 Ibid. 719

21 "Equity may give relief against contractual terms in a mortgage transaction if they are

oppressive or unconscionable"

22 B. McFarlane, Land Law (Oxford: Oxford University Press, 2017) p. 281

23 Ibid p. 286

Made in the USA
Columbia, SC
07 September 2020

18047742R00072